THE SOCIAL CONTEXT OF THE MAU MAU MOVEMENT IN KENYA (1952-1960)

Kinuthia Macharia
and Muigai Kanyua

University Press of America,® Inc.
Lanham · Boulder · New York · Toronto · Oxford

Copyright © 2006 by
University Press of America,® Inc.
4501 Forbes Boulevard
Suite 200
Lanham, Maryland 20706
UPA Acquisitions Department (301) 459-3366

PO Box 317
Oxford
OX2 9RU, UK

Library of Congress Control Number: 2005937941
ISBN 0-7618-3389-7 (paperback : alk. ppr.)

∞™ The paper used in this publication meets the minimum
requirements of American National Standard for Information
Sciences—Permanence of Paper for Printed Library Materials,
ANSI Z39.48—1984

Dedicated to the memory of Njeri Macharia and Muigai Kanyua

Table of Contents

Preface and Acknowledgements

For many years, I have been preoccupied with deep thoughts of how my life would have been different had my father (and for that matter, many other fathers who were detained or killed because of their participation in the Mau Mau Movement) had been left free to pursue his normal life. I am among many ex-Mau Mau detainees' children who were left to be raised by their mothers, luckily for some of us, temporarily (on average two to ten years). The mothers were usually afraid and not sure of whether they would ever see their husbands again. They were harassed by the authorities to "disclose more of" their husbands, they were equally harassed by their relatives; especially in the families they had married. They were usually regarded as a burden. I was then (late 1950s) youngest of three children when my father was detained and for four years, I only knew my Mom, who raised me despite the hardships of the time. I thank her dearly for the dedication. I met my father when I was four and I still remember refusing his warm gestures, as he was a "stranger" to me. Indeed, he had to give me his colorful bowl, which he used for his meals in detention. I guess I was won over by his warm persistence and the colorful bowl. I still see the colors (blue, white and yellow) of that bowl which I thought was the biggest bowl in the whole wide world. My mother used to talk more about the Mau Mau. She even taught me many of the Mau Mau songs, especially those that castigated the loyalists (like the dreaded ruthless home guards). As for my father, he did not want to talk much about it: I guess because of the suffering (physical and mental) that he had gone through, he wished to forget about it. There were times later in the years I could push him to tell me about it using the excuse of school—that we were studying the subject and I needed to hear from him in order to write a good report. He was not very open until later in the years when he could talk a little bit, especially if he was in the company of former Mau Mau detainees. It called for a nice social hour and good company to hear much about my father's involvement in the Movement. My mother, however, had told me much about his participation, initially as community leader in the "Reserves" who organized the food supply chain from the reserves to the forest. He was later accused of being the Mau Mau ringleader in Kariara location and especially in our local village of Kigoro. My mother used to tell me of how he was at one time beaten so hard in broad daylight by the local home guards and almost left for dead! Indeed to this day, his age-mates remember vividly the day he was physically beaten so hard.

My mother also told me (and this has been corroborated by others) of how he was taken to "Kwa Mwanya" (Special Area) to be killed. He was asked to dig his own grave, but, miraculously for him, the white soldier who aimed the gun in his "ready open grave" missed him. The white soldier told him that he must have been worshipping a very powerful god for he has never missed in shooting the target before. The white soldier decided not to aim again and it was after this incident that my father was detained in Manyani, later on in Mariira and then Kandara, just before he was finally freed. When my father was in a very happy mood and he wanted to recall the most courageous men he had ever met, he used to tell me of General Kago, who is discussed in the narrative below. He told me of how General Kago was so courageous to the extent that he was almost wild. He remembered vividly and narrated how he slapped him very hard because he hesitated to answer a question concerning food supply in Mbugiti! My father was not bitter later in the years talking about General Kago's hard slap on his face as he saw it as "a part of the struggle" and he was his superior in the Movement! General Kago died, as the reader will see below, later in one of the battles near Kandara.

Many young children (growing up in the late1950s to mid-1960s) of the Ki-kuyu, Embu, Meru and a few other ethnic groups that were involved in the Mau Mau can recall vividly the kind of division that existed in their communities. This was amongst the former loyalists (chiefs, sub-chiefs and home guards) and those commoners identified with the Mau Mau. Even when hatred was not taught, it was obvious that friendship networks, marriage networks and even religious and economic networks were socially constructed depending on one's immediate past heritage and general political affiliation. There are still remnants of this, especially for those keenly guided by the socio-economic history of their communities. Indeed, and of interest to current and future scholars, political leadership dynamics in most of Central Province and among the Embu and Meru could be seen as coups and counter-coups between the former loyalists and those that were opposed to the colonial regime hence associated with the Mau Mau. I thank my late friend, Mukaru Ng'ang'a, who in many discussions we held on this subject, was always ready to show how the political field, especially in the former Murang'a district, was a replay of the social-political dynamics that were the basis of the Mau Mau Movement. As a historian, he could explain the build-ing of alliances between and amongst the loyalists and the "commoners" and this was always fascinating. I could not agree more with my late friend's ideas and indeed I advance the same here. I will, however, call for further research to establish the facts on the social and political dynamics of the former rivaling groups over time.

A section of this book, especially the narrative, could not have been possi-ble without the hand-written vernacular (Kikuyu) version that the late Muigai Kanyua handed to me in the early 1990s. He was unsure whether there was enough material for a book or whether what he had written from his memory in the forest was worthwhile. He knew me having been from the same village. He also knew that I was teaching in a university abroad (Harvard University at the time). He assumed that as a scholar I might be interested in looking at what he had written. I had told him then I was busy finishing up my first book, besides my teaching obligations, and I could not promise when I could get to it. He was in no hurry and did not mind how long I took. He had, however, given me his blessings on the usage of his hand written Kikuyu notes in whichever way I found relevant. I could tell, though, his joy would be if I was able to make this into a book as he wanted to reach many readers. I had told him clearly there was no way I could give promises on that, as it is a tedious journey, as most authors would agree. Unfortunately he fell sick and passed on before I had even looked at his hand-written notes closely. After he passed on, I felt an obligation to make this a labor of love, first in his memory as his interest really was to tell the story of the forest first-hand to many people. With my earlier interest in the subject and with the theoretical framework of the "social movement," I got motivated to start translating into English his Kikuyu version. I have left most of it unchanged for the reader to get the experience, as the late Muigai would have wished. I thank him dearly for having been sensitive enough to document some of his experiences as it gives us a close look especially on events in the forest in the Nyandarua forest ridges. It also highlights the involvement of Muranga Mau Mau fighters, which is not as well documented as is that of the Nyeri and Mt. Kenya areas. I wish he had lived to see the final product in the form of this book. His contribution also emphasizes the need for education for all! If it were not for the little education he had acquired at Githunguri before the Independent schools were closed by the colonial regime, he would not have been able to document his memories in the forest. His, like many others' (for example my father's), would have been an "oral story" which may not have reached as many people as the "written story"! There are many times I have been tempted to abandon this project. I, however, felt I owed it to him, to my father and to many others that were tortured and died while fighting for what they truly believed was their freedom, their stolen lands as well as abuse of their human rights and humiliation by the colonial regime. I cannot thank him enough and that explains why I dedicate this book to him.

This book, then, is about the experiences of the Mau Mau fighters in the forest, especially those in the Nyandarua (formerly Aberdares Mountains) at the edge of what is today Gatanga and Maragua constituencies. It also has the academic goal of re-analyzing the Mau Mau from a social movement perspective. I argue that local organization in the communities for both women and men were critical to sustaining the movement for the almost ten years (1952-1962) that it dominated lives of many Kenyans, especially those in Nairobi Central and Eastern Provinces.

I want to thank others around me who have encouraged and stimulated me intellectually, especially my colleagues at Harvard whom I shared my thoughts on the Mau Mau and who encouraged me to pursue them—Profs. Peter Marsden, Mary Waters, Orlando Paterson and Stanley Lieberson. The latter at times made this a pet subject over many lunches we shared. I also used my graduate students at Harvard who took my seminar on Social Movements to test my ideas of looking at the Mau Mau from a social movement perspective. At American University, my colleagues, especially the former chair, Prof. Kenneth Kusterer, encouraged me to move this project; Prof. Esther Chow kept on reminding me about this project; and Prof. Bette Dickerson provided a stable environment during her days as chair besides being overall very supportive and a dear colleague. The collegial respect at American University and the responsive students have helped inspire me as well as move this project to the end product that it is in now. The College of Arts and Sciences through the Mellon Fellowship supported my research while doing this project. I have also benefited from friends who are also academics who will always ask me what I am working on. Prof. Charles Green takes the gold medal for having been there for me in all areas (private and public). Prof. Joe Lugalla, as well Makoba Wagona, have kept an interest on what I am doing and have sent me references or quotations which have overall enriched my work. I thank you.

One of my students, Kianda Bell, has been part of the "final touch finishing team" as he provided expertise especially in ensuring the bibliography and all the references have been inserted properly. I thank you and, hopefully, with your first name originating from the Kikuyus, you probably were able to identify with them as you read some of the chapters. At UPA I want to thank Beverly Baum who has been patient with me throughout the whole process.

My family has given me the stability I need and even when things have been rough, their encouragement has seen me through. My late wife, Njeri, was very supportive and even offered to translate the Kikuyu notes and was always fascinated with the idea of "the book." My wife, Alice, has been reminding me now and again that I need to finish "that book" and she has given me the support and the right atmosphere not only to finish "this book" but to embark on the next one! I thank you!

Finally, on behalf of all the children and the families of those who were involved in the Mau Mau Movement, especially those who were fighting directly or indirectly the colonial regime and its establishments, I thank you for your selfless commitment to make Kenya a better place for us and the generations to come!

Kinuthia Macharia
Washington, D.C.
April 18, 2005

Chapter 1

Introduction

The argument that will be emphasized in this chapter and throughout the book is that "social action" is both "economic and political action." I will show that in order to appreciate all the aspects of the Mau Mau "revolt," "rebellion" or Movement, as I will prefer to call it, the social map in Kenya in the late 1940s and the early 1950s should be understood. There has been so much emphasis on the political contribution of the Movement. I will explore the social contribution that led to the unity amongst people of different clans and ethnic groups. This was mainly necessitated by various oaths that those who were members of the Mau Mau took, for example the "oath of Unity." I will also explore the social disunity that this may have contributed in the heartland of the Kikuyu country where most of the Mau Mau activities took place. The disunity I refer to here was amongst those that did not take the oath of unity or any other, or the few who took it and later on turned their backs to become persecutors of their own brothers and sisters and of course former friends. This is one aspect in the Mau Mau literature that tends to be ignored, yet we find it a concern amongst those who were fighting in the forest. Truly, in the big picture, the Mau Mau fighters in the forest and in the reserves identified the "white man" ("nyakeru") or the British colonial ruler as their enemy No. 1. They also, however, had bitterness and were indeed looking forward to revenge against those that had turned to be supporters of the government. These were mainly those appointed as chiefs, sub-chiefs (headmen, as they were known then) and the notorious home guards that appeared to enjoy the miseries of the poor Mau Mau fighters, taking their land and their women and preaching doom.

There is the common tale, for example, of a Senior Chief who had to break up his radio on the eminence of Jomo Kenyatta's release. The story (now a legend) told by many adult villagers around Kigumo and Kandara divisions narrated how the Senior Chief had believed the propaganda of the colonial government which on a daily basis announced over the radio that "Kenyatta will never come back; there will never be a government headed by an African." When circa 1961 the radio announced that Kenyatta would be released, the illiterate Senior Chief who had all along taken the announcements of the radio as gospel truth dismantled it cursing it for having deceived him all those years that Kenyatta would never come back. The "radio" had also told him that the Mau Mau detainees would never be released. For him to hear that those detained would be allowed back in their homes was unimaginable as he had truly believed the white man was there to stay and the comfortable position he and his family occupied would continue unchecked for ever or at least in his lifetime. This is an aspect of social disunity that was the order of the day in the 1950s and early 1960s between the loyalists and the non-loyalists, the latter who formed the backbone of the Mau Mau.

The social impact of the disunity described above, which I argue has gone on for many years unaddressed by scholars can indeed help explain the social structure (based on class, clan and later on ethnicity) in present day Kenya. Thus to argue that a Social Movement has a life, that it is born and grows with time is to situate the Mau Mau Movement in a life span from the 1940s to the present.

It is within the context of the movement as an organism that I will situate the social context of the Mau Mau Movement from the past to the present. The international influences then and now will be discussed to show that movements do not happen in strict isolation or in a social vacuum. The effects of global process in the past ten years have indeed enhanced the cry of social justice worldwide. I will, for example, show how the pro-democracy and multi-party movements in most Third World countries have learned lessons from the past (like from the Mau Mau) and also from the present with such coverage of the Tiananmen Square Chinese student demonstrations, the Chiapas Movement in Mexico etc. The modern day instant coverage of such events not only inspires other oppressed people but gives them needed courage to organize themselves. The glory of the past and the practical knowledge of the present have indeed kept social movements alive in different parts of the world.

Although the Mau Mau Movement's most marked active years are 1952-1958, this period marks only the militant violent years of the movement. It also marks a big chunk of the time the narrator/Mau Mau participant describes in the following chapters. It is important to note that there were different branches of Mau Mau activities and participants. As Furedi (1991) argues, there were the politically advanced participants who tried to project the nationalist purpose for the Movement. These were primarily based in Nairobi and included the likes of Jomo Kenyatta, a nationalist politician who was not quite as involved in the grassroots organization of the Mau Mau as the colonialists mistakenly thought. These operated in Nairobi and perpetuated the need to negotiate with the colonial administration to address the problems faced by the Africans. They continued the quest for equality and return of the lands that had been addressed by the outlawed political parties dating back from Kikuyu Central Association (KCA) (1928) to Kenya African Union (KAU) (in the 1940s). Among these were political ideologues, some radical like Kaggia and Kubai (Kaggia 1975) and others less so like Kenyatta, who did not advocate violence and indeed denounced Mau Mau, especially the militant part of the movement.

There was also the branch of the squatters (Furedi 1991; Kanogo 1987; Throup 1987), especially those in the Rift Valley, the so-called White Highlands. These were fertile lands in the highlands of Kenya that were occupied by white settlers who vehemently believed it was their legitimately acquired land in contradiction with the indigenous populations who had always perceived this land as their God-given rightfully achieved possession. As we will see below one of the fueling grievances dating back before the violent part of the movement was the "cry for land" which went unanswered, leaving many landless people juxtaposed against the landed settlers and those of the Kikuyu establishment loyal to the colonialists. The squatters as Kanogo (1987) and Furedi (1991) noted were Kikuyu who had earlier moved to the Rift Valley, fleeing from the congested ancestral Central Province which had become congested with population. The fertile land had been taken and transformed into coffee and tea, pineapple, and sisal plantations by the white settlers. The Kikuyu had been forced to share land in the so-called Kikuyu Reserve. Due to over-cultivation and lack of money to add fertilizers and manure to the land, the soils had become barren yielding inadequate crops. Famine became the order of the day in Central Province Kikuyu Reserve, a fact of life that was also shared by those in the forest as is shown in the latter part of this book. These reserves had been transformed from one-time granary of the Kikuyu to brown-patched overused soils that could not feed the growing population. In the height of colonial rile and during the Mau Mau Movement, Malthus' (1798) theory of population, where population would overtake food supply, could have been easily tested, passing with flying colors. The theory could be reversed today or after independence when the farmers were able to fertilize their land and do rotational cropping to bring back the high yields, ending the kinds of famine that were present during the period of the 1950s to early 1960s. It is as a result of such famine and congestion that some Kikuyu out-migrated from the Central Province to the Rift Valley. For about two decades, 1930s-1950s, the Kikuyu squatters in the Rift Valley led good lives. Even though most of them were farm hands for the colonial settlers, there was abundance of land, and they were allowed to keep their own livestock and grow their own crops, which they could sell and make extra money. They were comparatively better off than their relatives residing in Central Province. As the militant phase of the Mau Mau Movement got in motion, restrictions as to how much they could cultivate and more forced labor were put in place. In their efforts to keep the Rift Valley free of the "radicalized Kikuyu," the colonial administration started a program that required the Rift Valley squatters to return to their original homes in Central Province at once. This forced relocation and loss of property (homes, crops and livestock) was not taken kindly. It led many of those squatters who were young and able to join the militant wing of the Mau Mau in the Nyandarua Mountains instead of going back to poverty in Central Province. These former squatters formed their own guerrilla wing that terrorized the white settlers and their loyalists in the Naivasha-Njabi-ini areas. General Mbaria mentioned below led one such military wing of former squatters in the Nyandudo section of the Aberdares (Nyandarua Mountains near the present day Wanjohi). The humiliating forced exodus from their warm habitats back to the now socially distant Central Province was unfathomable to the Rift Valley squatters. This explains their agitation and the choice for many to join the militant Mau Mau wing instead of enduring further humiliation, movement restriction and the degrading "villigization program" that was already in place in Central Province.

The loyalists in the Kikuyu Reserve were also able to acquire more land at the expense of their own brothers and sisters. That division was to lead to the third branch of Mau Mau activists/participants who indeed formed the bulk of those who used the forest of the Aberdares (Nyandarua) and Mt. Kenya as their locations of operation. The forest became home to thousands of young Kikuyu militants who were mostly descendants of the peasantry in Central Province (Itote 1967; Njama 1966). The peasantry in the districts of Murang'a, Kiambu and Nyeri felt they had nothing to lose except their humiliation and poverty, hence the willy-nilly move to the forest that became the choice for most young people. It is notable that within Central Province among the Kikuyu establishment, the loyalists supported the colonial administration so vehemently that most of the violence within the Kikuyu Reserve was usually the militant defiant peasantry against the loyalists. The latter had favors from the colonial administration in the form of orchestrated economic and social power.

They were usually the appointed chiefs, the headmen and the homeguards. They were able to acquire more land and to humiliate those who were not loyal to the colonial administration. Kaggia (1975) notes how the loyalists took away from his family's fertile land while he was away in prison, having been imprisoned in 1952 on the eve of the militant part of the Mau Mau. He was left with only a rocky barren land, which was much less productive. The favoritism that the Kikuyu loyalists got from the administration distanced them socially and economically from the poor peasantry as evidenced in the D. Mukaru Ng'ang'a (1981) article confirming the advantages the loyalists gained in Murang'a in the late 1950s and early 1960s. They obtained favorable decisions during land consolidation by their participation in coffee societies and by obtaining loans for agricultural development.

The loyalist ironically had a head start on economic and social participation at the expense of their peasantry counterparts (Sandgren 1989). The latter were either still in the forest or in detention until the early 1960s. This explains why the gap between the loyalists in Central Province and the peasantry in terms of socio-economic status has never been narrowed to date. Indeed an analysis of the present day socio-economic stratification in Central Province in particular and Kenya in general may only be understood from a historical materialism perspective. As Marx (1887) had earlier noted, the history of ownership of property and control of ideas and knowledge is as important today as it was in the past to explain class locations of a given society. This could not be truer than in Central Province of Kenya, where the Mau Mau activities were most felt and where early inclusion of the Kenya economy into the capitalist system was mostly active. It is the sons and daughters of the loyalists (chiefs, headmen and homeguards) who were more likely to be educated in the few government schools in Central Province. The parents could afford to pay the school fees and their children were not labeled as descendants of the Mau Mau, hence they experienced a more conducive learning environment than those of the peasants. It is no wonder that most of these sons and daughters of the former loyalists, their friends or those associated by marriage were able to fill in key government positions after independence and the socio-economic gap has continued to widen. While things may be changing in the last ten years, the trend has been that the descendants of the former loyalists tend to have more inherited land property, generally are more educated and, as such, are in most of the key leadership positions locally and nationally.

This third branch of the Mau Mau could therefore be further subdivided between the peasantry who took arms in the forest and the peasantry who were in the Reserve. The latter were equally important in the Movement, as they were the main suppliers of food and medicine, as well as information about the enemy, which was just as important. They tended to be more humiliated by the colonial administration, particularly by the loyalists. They were interrogated and punished so as to confess having taken the secret oath that united all Mau Mau activists/participants. The chiefs and their cronies also forced them into the degrading communal labor, which involved digging terraces to control soil erosion in government lands and those privately owned by the white settlers and the loyalists. They were also forced to dig with hoes in lieu of tractors to make roads that the colonial administration vehicles could use to penetrate the interior of the Reserve. Further, they were the ones who adhered to the enforced curfew hours of 6:00 a.m. to 6:00 p.m.

With the humiliating program (1956-1963) of "villigization" (i.e., moving every Kikuyu from their ancestral lands to a centralized location) with fences (some electric) and a gate so as to make direct colonial administration more effective, they had to bear the brunt of being herded together like a flock of sheep or unruly school children. The British had experimented with this program in Malaya (Malaysia) and in their minds it was an effective way of controlling "ruddy and disobedient natives." For the Kikuyu, as was with the people of Malaya, this was the worst form of control—feeling dehumanized and being denied one's identity, especially losing control of one's traditional home and small farm. Most did not like being separated from their livestock that they held dearly and which was close to their daily routine and world-view. The centralized villages were generally divided into six sections: 1) the common village, with the young and the middle aged; 2) the elderly (what may be referred to as senior citizens in the United States); 3) the loyalists section which accommodated the headmen and the home guards; 4) a section of administration police, commonly referred to as the "post" or "bothiti" in gikuyu; 5) a section where livestock, especially cattle and sheep, was housed; and 6) a small section where there was a shop or two and possibly one small dingy restaurant serving mainly tea and toast.

A collective action out of the humiliation endured by these different branches of the activists/participants had been developing within the Central African Reserve, the nationalists in Nairobi and the squatters in Central Province. The colonial state-building in the form of Bura-Matari (the rock crasher) as referred to in Congo (Young 1985) was in direct contradiction and conflict with the wishes of the Africans in the Kenya colony. That conflict and the need for collective action leading to a militant operation in the form of the Mau Mau became inevitable in the early fifties. So long as one was a Kikuyu in the early fifties and throughout that decade, whether in the Rift Valley, in the Reserve or in the towns like Nairobi, the colonial administration was set up "to round up and tame the radical Kikuyu." The "Operation Anvil," where all Kikuyu were rounded up, humiliated and repatriated back to their original homes or Reserve, was the climax of such anti-Kikuyu schemes by the colonial authorities. They were seen as the bad seeds of discord that were about to rock the peace and tranquility of the colonial settlers in their beloved Kenya colony. This could not be allowed as it was seen as a sure way to colonial economic demise. It should also be noted that the British were at this time losing other colonies, especially in Asia, for example, where the Malaya were already defiant and in arms and India had already gotten their independence in 1947. In other words, what was happening even in as distant places as Malaya and India was having an indirect impact on the fueling of the Mau Mau Movement in Kenya. This goes to show that movements do not take place in a social-political or regional vacuum. What may be happening elsewhere may directly impact on the path the organization of a movement may take. The rounding up and total dismantling of the Kikuyu socio-economic life became the motto of the colonial administrators and their loyal followers. The punitive program to bring the Kikuyu "under control" meant total disruption of cultural practices. For example, festivals were outlawed, religious activities were outlawed and the Kikuyu Independent Churches and schools were banned. This impacted on young students who had the desire to have an education. They were forced to make a choice of going to the Reserve and suffering humiliation that their parents were already going through or alternatively going to the forest to join the militant wing of the Mau Mau.

The main story that follows in this book shows, among other things, a case of an aspiring student who had to make the difficult choice of going into the forest against his grandiose hopes and wishful thinking. He had dreamt and worked towards one day becoming a university student in Makerere, then the University of East Africa. The wishes of many young middle aged and old Kikuyu men were destroyed, and for many never to be realized again either by themselves or their offspring. The situation was worse for the women who had a lower social-economic status than the men. They were put in a much lower one with the new economic order of plantation employment and militant face of the Mau Mau which made the situation more of a "man's world" than a "woman's world." This came with a big price for the women. Many of them became impoverished and had to take up what were formerly men's roles when their husbands were either taken to prison or moved into the forest to join the Kenya Freedom Army (popularly referred to as the Mau Mau fighters). This is part of the story you are about to read, but before you do that, I will put the Mau Mau Movement in a theoretical framework highlighting more the "social" in it than just the "economic," the "political" and the "historical." These disciplinary analyses have tended to take center stage amongst previous scholars on the subject (see, for example, Kanogo 1987; Lonsdale 1991; Maloba 1992; Odhiambo 1988, 1999; Rosberg and Nottingham 1966; Throup 1987).

Chapter 2

What Makes Mau Mau a Social Movement?

In this chapter, I will discuss the relevant theories that explain social movements in general and specifically those that can analyze the "social" in the Mau Mau Movement. Social movements in general have been defined as conscious, organized, and collective actions to bring about or resist social change (Piven and Cloward 1979; West and Blumberg 1990). This definition encompasses many such movements—workers' rights and trade union movements, for example, that were at their apogee in the United States during the 1930s. It also includes movements towards national liberation and getting rid of the colonial yoke, as was the case in the 1950s in Asia and Africa.

Social movements vary in organization and purpose. Some form of collective behavior (Smelser 1962) will usually be expected for an action to qualify as a social movement, hence the need to mobilize and to have some goals or purpose. Good leadership will usually be suggestive of how successful a movement might be and whether it realizes the goals of those identifying themselves as members. Early scholars of mass action (Le Bon 1982) did not identify legitimacy in movements and described such collective behavior as a form of panic, mindlessness and an action that may call for social psychological therapy. The field of collective behavior is central to ideas of early sociologists who were particularly interested in the influence of the group on the individual. Founding fathers of sociology (Comte, Durkheim, Spencer) were all concerned about this issue and indeed represented what was seen as a revolt against individualistic explanations of human social behavior based on "reason" or "sensations." These early philosopher-sociologists felt that psychology, with its emphasis on individual analysis, did not adequately explain human social behavior. It was along that same line of reasoning that Comte argued that the family, not the individual, was the true social unit and that the mind could develop only in a social state. His writing stimulated interest in the group and in social interaction, particularly among French scholars of the time, notably, Emile Durkheim (1956), with his study of social action and the emphasis of the "group over the individual," a key distinction to date of the discipline of Sociology. It is no wonder that sometimes Durkheim is considered a "group mind theorist" for helping create a situation in which he showed the importance of group influence over individual behavior. We can extend this early thinking to recent ideas as we focus on how collective behavior comes about and its significance in contributing to change.

Among the early French social thinkers who contributed to the study of the group (collective behavior) is Gustave Le Bon (1982). He is often identified as the founder of collective behavior. He wrote about the "psychology of the crowd" and presented the crowd as the prototype of all group behavior. Le Bon's interest in the crowd which he at times described as having mindless behavior, mostly well represented in a riot situation, differs from later theorists, especially those emphasizing the rationality of groups in their quest for change. Theorists like McAdam (1992) and Smelser (1962) would agree that collective behavior, which may be a response to social strain, could be well orchestrated and rational and not in the least mindless as Le Bon described it. Interestingly and of relevance to the Mau Mau Movement is the fact that the British colonial interpretation of the Mau Mau was in line with Le Bon's ideas, as they saw those heralding the Mau Mau as being mindless and psychologically lacking in their actions and goals. Of course, this was not true as has been argued before (Rosberg and Nottingham 1966) and as I will also argue in this book. The legitimacy of the Mau Mau followers was suppressed, especially by the white settlers who were determined to settle forever in Kenya enforcing white supremacy of governance and culture (i.e., be modern, Christian, emulate white ways while abandoning African "primitive traditions" and, of course, be engaged as insignificant co-opted actors in a predominantly-run European economy. For the white settlers and the colonial government at the time, in Kenya, any grievances voiced by the Africans was ignored and met with utter punishment. Indeed, the senselessness in which the African's genuine grievances were met not only fueled the fires that ultimately produced the Mau Mau Movement and war but also in retrospect shows how senseless the settlers and the colonial establishment were in Kenya. From the 1920s when Kikuyu Central Association was formed (1924) to the late 1940s when the actual speeding up towards the Mau Mau Movement was being organized with the eminence of war in the early 1950s, the Africans had articulated their grievances. Unfortunately, they were either ignored as irrelevant or inconsequential, and this would ultimately cause strain between the white supremacy and the African forced inferiority status. This form of social-political-economic strain has been established to be an almost inevitable necessity leading to the emergence of a social movement (Smelser 1962) and evidently this was the case for the Mau Mau in Kenya.

The major unanswered grievances that led to the Mau Mau Movement include the following:

1. Land—this was the most critical of all the grievances. The Kikuyu people in Central Province felt in particular that their land had been encroached and taken without their permission or proper compensation. There are those who have argued that most of the land settled by the white farmers was indeed Maasai or Kalenjin land (Ogot 1992) and little of the Kikuyu land was stolen. The fact of the matter is that the Kikuyu had already started expanding from their original district of Murang'a, southward to Kiambu (Leakey 1977) and northwards to Nyeri towards Laikipia (Nanyuki area), well before the coming of the white settlers. Their expansion was curtailed with the new settler occupation, and they were confined in what was referred to as the Kikuyu Reserve, which had been cultivated for many years and, since the population had been expanding, the lands there were barren and exhausted from many years of cultivation. The Kikuyu mythology believed that land was freely given to them by the Mwene-Nyaga, Ngai (their god who dwelled on top of Kirinyaga (Mt. Kenya) (Kenyatta 1938). It was theirs to keep and to cultivate to feed their children and not to be taken away by foreigners. This belief by itself was enough to want to fight the foreigners, especially when they could not listen or grant such an important grievance. Indeed, it is clear that the cry for land was so important that it mobilized the young and the old to come together and form a formidable force that eventually became violent pressing on the same demands—getting their land back! Social mobilization is a key element of any social movement (McAdam 1982; McCarthy and Zald 1996; Tarrow 1996). The cry and quest for stolen land was such an agent of mobilization among the Kikuyu, fostered by their belief that their land was indeed stolen and re-enforced by traditional beliefs, that they had to defend their Ngai—God-given land. It is within this context that the oaths taken by those Kikuyu who joined the Movement should be understood—not as atavistic, but genuine mobilization effects which eventually led to the Movement that was to be labeled Mau Mau. It should be understood that land as a grievance was so serious that it was enough to lead to the violence that the colonial government may not have anticipated from these poorly armed and peaceful people, as the Kikuyu were previously described (Leakey 1977).

2. Forced Labor—The encroachment of the Kikuyu land led to the eventual forced labor phenomenon whereby the white Europeans who got the land needed laborers to work on the stolen land and make it productive. Various ways to bring about this phenomenon were employed, the

key among them being the introduction of poll and hut taxes. The taxes were to be paid in cash and the Kikuyu therefore were forced to work in order to earn the cash to pay for the taxes. With the stolen land and rising population, it also meant that the Kikuyu Reserve were becoming too congested to the extent that the more able-bodied men and women had to leave to look for work in the newly-acquired white lands—so called the "White Highlands"! This explains the movement of Kikuyus from Central Province (their traditional region) to the Rift Valley where many ended up being (Furedi 1991; Kanogo 1987). There was also the forced "communal labor," especially in the 1950s, which was enforced on families to make rural roads and water catchment facilities as well as the unpopular terraces that were dug on farms to protect soil erosion. The local chiefs and home guards supervised the communal forced labor which was punitive and outright unpopular (interview with author's mother who resented the communal labor, especially because she was pregnant with me and later when I was still an infant was expected to keep the enforced hours). The women and children suffered most since they were expected to keep up the communal labor schedule and observe the enforced curfew (dawn to dusk), whereby they were expected to be back in the now (1954-1960) enclosed and heavily guarded villages. In between, they were expected to also make time to cultivate their gardens for their daily food. As we can see from the narration which follows (Chapters 4-12), some of these people in the Reserve also discreetly supported those Mau Mau men and women in the forest by securing food, medicine, clothes and other essentials for the forest fighters. The mobilization of this Movement did not cease at the identification of those entering the forest. It continued in the Reserve, and this energy sustained the movement for the many years it survived. "Forced labor" was thus a grievance that once not heeded by the colonial powers and the white settlers mobilized those who entered the forest to fight. This grievance also mobilized protest for those who were left behind who continued to be brutalized and forced to work for free in the local government projects as well as in the neighboring coffee plantations owned by the white settlers.

3.   Humiliation and Abuse of Human Rights—The Kikuyu men and women felt humiliated by the oppressive colonial laws. This was partly as an accumulation of being ignored as they raised the first two grievances addressed above. They felt as if they were treated with no dignity, with grown men and women being compared to children. Those working in settler farms were underpaid and given food with rations that were not enough for the families. They were constantly verbally abused and punished in public in case the white settlers thought they had done something "wrong." When poll and hut taxes were introduced, for example, the colonial administration, through local chiefs

and police, raided homes either very early in the mornings or in the evenings (about nightfall) and chased those who may not have paid. It was like a hunting spree for wildlife, but this time it was for the men targeted to pay taxes. House goods could be confiscated and forcibly sold to pay for the taxes when the owner of the home (hut) had fled away. The treatment from the colonial administration was totally lacking in dignity. This grievance was raised in various forums but fell onto deaf ears. This led the Kikuyu to organize themselves and mobilize the youth and the elders to form committees that eventually would prepare those who joined the Movement.

4. Racism ("Color-Bar")—Discrimination of all sorts (based on color, gender and tribal affiliation) was particularly leveled against the Kikuyu much more than any other ethnic group in Kenya. That kind of direct discrimination triggered dissent, and when the concerns were voiced, again they fell on deaf ears. In particular, the African soldiers, among them Kikuyu men like Bildad Kaggia (Kaggia 1975), who had served with the British army during the Second World War in such places as Burma and Egypt, decried the fact that they had served abroad and had certain privileges while serving but were discriminated against on the basis of their color when they returned. As black people for example, they were not supposed to consume bottled beer (a preserve for Europeans) and this angered these World War II veterans who had liked the taste of bottled beer while serving outside Kenya. The schools were also run on color lines, those of the Europeans (white) being the best and the Africans (black) being the worst and few in numbers. The political and bureaucratic power based on one's color was also a reality for Africans, especially Kikuyu who were in close proximity with the white settlers and administration had to deal with on a daily basis. Racist attitudes and laws led to powerlessness among the Kikuyu. The black powerlessness in their own land was a grievance raised at every opportunity the Kikuyu had—through the local chiefs and churches—but it was not heeded. It would eventually lead to mobilization for the Movement.

5. Cultural Deprivation and Discrimination—Regardless of how weak a group of people is, when deprived and discriminated, cultural pride amongst them leads to different forms of resistance. The Kikuyu had raised concerns that the white missionaries and administration did not respect their culture. The climax of this was when the white church leaders collaborated with the colonial administration to outlaw circumcision for girls—a ritual that was so dear and seen as core to the Kikuyu culture. It had led earlier into defiance climaxed by the Muthirigu dance (a dance performed to directly protest missionary and government directives against female circumcision) (Sandgren 1989). Tradi-

tional beliefs and customs were discriminated against in favor of the so-called modern Christian ways, as evidently depicted in Ngugi wa Thiong'o's novel, *The River Between* (Wa Thoing'o 1965). The divisions caused by this selective discrimination of traditional culture in the Kikuyu country were to such an extent that by the time of the Mau Mau Movement turning violent, there were two distinct camps (the loyalists and the non-loyalists) based on one's position on the cultural changes that were taking place. Those who felt their culture was being discriminated and deprived were ready to be mobilized to go to the forest and fight for both their lost land and what was also perceived as their "soon-to-be-lost culture"! It is not surprising, therefore, that when a group of people feel their culture is being discriminated against or it is being deprived of its core, at such time as the social movement eventually gains momentum, as in the case of the Mau Mau, the cultural practices that were being discriminated against will feature in the form of protest. Indeed the cultural apparatus of the group will feature prominently and will give character to the movement. This may explain why the Mau Mau Movement was heavily characterized by Kikuyu culture (oaths, songs and even killing methods using the panga (long knife) as the basic weapon to attack the enemy). Aldon Morris (1986), in his analysis of the Civil Rights Movement, emphasizes the structure of Southern Black communities and aspects of Black culture that developed under conditions of oppression. The Gikuyu culture in Mau Mau dominated, just like the Southern Black culture dominated the Civil Rights Movement of the 1960s in the United States. Other theorists, like McAdam and Rucht (1993) in their research on protest repertoires, link culture and micro-structural relations by tracing the diffusion of collective action frames via social networks. It is not surprising that the Kikuyu had to utilize their social networks as reinforcement for their systematic protest, which led to the Mau Mau Movement. Such social networks that were utilized for the build-up of the Mau Mau Movement included the "riika," age-mates who were usually assembled together as a group to take certain oaths that reinforced the belief and commitment to the Movement; and gender networks (men and women organized as varied social groups with specific expectations of each of them). Clans also were the basis of social networks that were utilized by those who re-enforced the growth of the Mau Mau Movement. It became quite a problem in areas where some clan members had converted to Christianity or had become loyalists by having been appointed chiefs or home guards. This created a schism amongst clan members throughout the life of the Mau Mau Movement (1952-1960). Unfortunately the realities of that schism are still observed to date where certain clans will not intermarry because of the position various clan members took during the Mau Mau Movement. It also strikes a nerve especially in modern capitalist Kenya where the children of the former loyalists continue to do well in material accumulation at the expense of the children of the former Mau Mau activists, participants and, particularly, the forest fighters. Thus, social movements are not just shaped by culture. They also shape culture or reshape it. The Mau Mau Movement shaped a culture of protest against various forms of discrimination by government authorities. Such protests have at times resurfaced against the government of the day when people feel so discriminated as was the case during the colonial powers and the Mau Mau. University students have protested, workers have protested and those who feel their land is being taken away from them have also protested. At the end of the Mau Mau Movement, a call by some of the leaders for reconciliation was heard, and it was expected to be the basis of a new Kikuyu order given the fact that the old order had really been destroyed by the Mau Mau Movement. Many strides to reconcile former warring groups were taken and there was no open hostility. However, for those who are keen observers, subtle references to the old order still continue as those who were in the Mau Mau Movement and their descendants still feel the injustice done to them during the colonial administration and also after independence by Kenyatta's and Moi's regime. Kibaki's regime is too new to be judged as to what overtures it will give to the former Mau Mau fighters and their descendants. This issue will be revisited in Chapter 13.

It is evident from the discussion above that some of the early theories (e.g., Le Bon's) that emphasized the breakdown in a social system or reactions to a destabilized system do not quite explain the situation with the Mau Mau Movement. Indeed we see the harsh treatment of the natives (Kikuyus specifically), the forced labor, forced taxes, lack of political representation, belittling the natives by equating them with children, etc. were all adequate grievances to lead to a social movement. Thus, theories associating the rise of movements wit an attempt to achieve denied opportunities are more relevant to the case of the Mau Mau (McCarthy and Zald 1973; Smelser 1963; Turner and Killian 1972). What was also evident in the Mau Mau Movement that is also characteristic with other social movements studied elsewhere is the power the movement gains over time, which also becomes a basis for recruitment of new members and retention of the old ones. The power in a movement according to Tarrow (1994) grows when ordinary people join forces in contentious confrontation with elites, authorities and opponents. Mau Mau Movement had that power. It drew from the ordinary, uneducated poor farmers who had a gargantuan task of overthrowing the colonial administration in Kenya to regain back their land and dignity. In such situations, people are drawn into collective action. At their base are social networks and cultural symbols through which social relations are organized. This may again be reemphasized for those trying to argue that the Mau Mau was not a national movement but a tribal one (Ochieng 1989; Ogot 1992). Local social networks and cultural symbols are necessary requirements to bring about a collective action that will lead to a successful and formidable movement to last the many years the Mau Mau did. Those local connections, cultural symbols and social networks become the motor that makes the engine of the social movement continue running. Compared with other great social movements (e.g., the Civil Rights Movement) there is nothing unusual for the Kikuyu cultural identity the Mau Mau Movement took! That did not make it any less national, as was the Civil Rights Movement which, while having an overwhelming Southern Black culture, was not considered a regional movement, but was indeed a national one! For those who have argued that the Mau Mau Movement was as a result of Kikuyu chauvinism (Lonsdale 1991; Ochieng 1989) they should (from the above discussion) understand that the Mau Mau Movement was triggered by colonial humiliation and oppression and not at all by Kikuyu chauvinism. The Kikuyu organized to fight for their unanswered grievances by the colonial establishment and its supporters (many of whom were fellow Kikuyu) and not against other ethnic groups in Kenya. The Kikuyu in the Mau Mau Movement indeed welcomed other ethnic groups who supported them, like the neighboring Kamba. They were clear as to who the enemy was and at no time were they imagining the enemy being any African ethnic group in Kenya. That is why the argument of Kikuyu chauvinism should be shelved, never to be retrieved, as it only blurs the truth of the Movement. Indeed the failure of the Movement to acquire national acceptance and recognition (although it had international recognition) was simply because of the aggressive "divide and rule policy" that was ingrained in the colonial administration. The clarity those in the Movement had as to who was the enemy was evidenced by the fact that they attacked the Kikuyu establishment that was pro-colonial (the loyalists, the chiefs and the home guards as well as the African police). They attacked them as they were part of the colonial establishment. To understand the situation that those joining the Mau Mau Movement found themselves, we may also borrow from Marx (1887) who argued that people will engage in collective action when their social class is fully developed in contradiction with its antagonists. I will be the first to admit that those joining the Mau Mau were not necessarily a developed class but they surely identified as a "class" when they all understood that they needed to retake their land back, were no longer going to succumb to humiliation and child-like treatment, etc. A form of collective action and consciousness in organizing and mobilizing for the movement ensued and indeed sustained it for at least ten years. The home guards, chiefs and other loyalists had a false consciousness, identifying themselves with the colonial administration and, as such, fighting against their fellow Kikuyus. The Mau Mau Movement was organized and led by ordinary people and not by professional revolutionaries as Lenin (1987) would have suggested. Nor were there any collective "intellectuals" as Gramsci (1971) would suggest. Indeed, Tarrow's argument of denial of political opportunities comes closest to defining Mau Mau best: a moment of organizing to regain such restricted and denied political opportunities.

The above theoretical discussion has shown and situated the Mau Mau as a social movement. The emphasis here is on the *"social"* especially the use of social networks, social cultural values, norms, etc. in organizing and sustaining the movement. The Mau Mau Movement should be studied like any other major social movement as it has the characteristics that identify a social movement. In the next chapter, the role of women and their contribution to the Mau Mau Movement will be discussed.

Chapter 3

Gender Roles and the Contribution of Women in the Mau Mau Movement

In this chapter, the gender roles among the Kikuyu society, particularly prior to the beginning of the Mau Mau Movement and the change during the course of the Movement, will be discussed. The hardships the women endured, especially those left behind as young brides, who became single mother overnight, will be discussed. The women's contribution in the combat zones, where Mau Mau battles were fought, and in intelligence gathering will be discussed. The chapter's purpose is to give the women in the Mau Mau Movement a more center stage than most works before this one have done, especially examining their important contribution to the Movement. The women made not only contribution in the combat zone, but also in many other important areas, including spying (Otieno 1998), transporting food and, more importantly, becoming the guardian of those left behind in the Reserve. They raised and nurtured the future Kikuyu sons and daughters of the Mau Mau. They also contributed economically to the agricultural production of what was left of Central Province and the neighboring settler farms where they had to work in harsh conditions, receiving poor pay for their own survival and that of their children.

Gender is a social construction. This means that the social roles that we do are not determined by our biological sex differences (male or female) but are as a result of the society in which we grow up and how we get socialized to act or think feminine or masculine. One may argue that gender roles need not be universal, rather should be particularistic to the specific society. While that is to a large extent true, there are some universal elements of socialization and these have tended to generate a gendered society with little variations in general between and amongst societies. One universal practice that tends to bring about a gendered form in many societies is patriarchy, the practice whereby males (men) tend to be in control of females (women). Men in such cases will have the upper hand in negotiating and formalizing women's roles, which will tend to be less attractive compared with the men's roles. Common sense would suggest that most of those in charge will tend to favor themselves and to ensure they have privileged positions compared with those that are under their control. Thus in many societies that are patriarchal, the tendency has been that women, by and large, have been controlled by men and have tended to be socialized to accept less important roles in their societies. In general, they would have no voice especially on war matters or confrontational political issues like the Mau Mau Movement that would become militant and bloody for many years. While this may be universal, in this chapter we will examine the extent it was true among the Kikuyu and what that patriarchal arrangement meant before and during the decade that dominated the Mau Mau Movement.

Social movements tend to reproduce the gender inequalities that already exist in a given society. A social movement is itself a microcosm of the larger society and it is not unusual to find the same divisions though some activists within a movement, especially one calling for social justice, may try to address notable inequalities. The Civil Rights Movement in the United States focused mainly on racial inequalities but, down the line, gender inequalities were raised as a concern by the activists. The Women's Movement in the United States could very well be seen as a continuum of the Civil Rights Movement. This is the unconscious impact of a socially dynamic movement, that is, issues of social justice being dealt with almost simultaneously even though they may not have been the primary subject.

The Kikuyu society was patriarchal before the coming of the white man. Men occupied the privileged "warrior" positions of the society and the women were mainly relegated to homemaking roles. This does not mean by any measure that the women were disrespected in the Kikuyu society. On the contrary, they controlled a lot of respect and were especially respected as custodians of homes (a home here meant a family—husband and children), but not quite the same as a Western family. Indeed a man who was of age and was not married was seen as lacking and did not command as much respect as when he got married. That partnership was respected as well as the important role women played as consultants, albeit in private, for many matters in which their husbands could have been involved. The Kikuyu had a Council of Elders (Kiama) as the highest decision-making body for the tribe. There would be selected council of elders in the fragmented Kikuyu society and a Kiama could represent one or two neighboring villages. The women could not participate in the Kiama, but it was commonly known that the men in the Kiama would privately consult their wives or their mothers. Thus, though publicly unacknowledged, privately, they made a contribution. In this regard, the Kikuyu conformed to many other societies based on the patriarchal arrangement where the woman's role is mainly in the private (home) domain while the man's is in the public domain (in this case the Kiama and the political participation that would lead to the Mau Mau Movement). The men tended to clear the virgin land for cultivation, but after planting (maize, beans, cassava bananas or potatoes) the women did the bulk of the work of maintaining the gardens. The men tended to be closely associated with the animals, especially cattle, sheep and goats—the women kept the chickens, which was seen as having little commercial value.

The women were busy most of the time as they had the gardens to attend to during the day and the home to maintain, itself a full-time job (day and night) and the young ones to tend to. The men had more time to themselves and some were almost idlers, especially after having done the main clearing work of a proposed "shamba," garden. They had more time to meet amongst themselves, share in conversations and drink together. The men had the first direct contact with the colonial regime, as they were the ones forcefully recruited for labor in the white settler farms. The men were also the ones who first felt the direct loss of their property in the form of confiscated land, and they were the ones who felt the first impact of paying the hut tax and the poll tax, both imposed on every adult male in Central Province— and later in other selected districts. Men, who apparently had more time to themselves and were more in the public sphere, became the agitators for their own human rights against the colonial regime. They felt oppressed by the colonial regime; however, they did not consider themselves as having been oppressing their women. They had been socialized that way and did not see the inequalities brought about by their privileged positions. When oppression, especially from an outsider, was directed to them, the men started organizing and engaging in political activism through the Kikuyu Central Association (KCA), formed in 1928 and, some time later, the Kenya African Union (KAU). These became forums of political activism heavily dominated by men. The fact that it was mainly the men who were recruited to assist the British during the Second World War also meant that men were more exposed publicly and when they came back after the war, they were more politicized and animated in their quest for equality and elimination of the colonial forms of oppression and discrimination. Most of the meetings to discuss the next course of action, especially that which led to the militant wing of the Mau Mau were held in Nairobi and were usually attended by men. I will, however, argue that these men who met had wives or women friends and they shared some of the issues discussed with them. They may not have been at the forefront but they had awareness of what was going on and they supported their men. They were silent partners in what was to become "a very loud movement."

When the men were organizing in the public sphere, we should not lose sight of the fact that the women were organizing, albeit more informally, and using informal networks in their homes—the private sphere. They were supporting their men; they were hiding the men's whereabouts when the government security/loyalists came to the homes to ask the whereabouts of their husbands, sons or friends. In other words, though not publicly acknowledged, the women were in the Mau Mau struggle right from its beginnings because, after all,, they were part of the society that was already conflicted. Kuumba (2001) criticizes rightly most of the mainstream theories that explain social movements but do not apply the gender lens, hence underplay the contribution of women in such movements. She criticizes the Political Process Model as well as the Resource Mobilization theories as having given lip service to women's roles. Instead, she advocates the Emergent Theory from Movement Lives which suggests that the theory of social movements should emerge organically from the experience of women and men in particular movements. Indeed, in the case of the Mau Mau, such women as Wambui Otieno (1998) and Muthoni Likimani (1985) are but a few of the women participants in the Mau Mau Movement who have told their story and place the women's contribution at the forefront, hence giving a gender balance in our understanding of the Movement.

The basis of the women's contributions is best told by the women themselves, especially those who participated in the Movement. In lieu of the fact that most of those who participated were of peasant stock and mostly uneducated—as was the case of my mother—oral narratives that my mother and other women in my home area told me and others will form the basis of the discussion below on the specific contributions that women made to the Movement. These women, now in their sixties and seventies remember the Mau Mau days of the 1950s as if they were yesterday. This is mainly because of the enormous suffering they endured in form of physical and verbal (psychological) torture, formal detentions and informal punishment, especially coping with their daily routines in an atmosphere of forced curfew of 6:00 a.m. to 6:00 p.m., which was enforced in Central Province and other areas like Meru and Embu where Mau Mau was deemed very active. The kind of physical and psychological torture that the women and the men endured has been detailed in Elkin (2005) who portrays the British torture of the Mau Mau as being equivalent to that of the Russian gulag. I cannot help but to cite one such incident of torture my mother told me: She was held night and day for three consecutive days immediately outside the entrance of a stinking latrine (a full one almost overflowing with human excrement) as a torture device because she could not tell of her husband's whereabouts. At that time my father was supposedly a fugitive who was needed to answer charges of participating in the Mau Mau, then a proscribed illegal movement. She told me of the cold nights and the strong stench especially on the hot windy days with flies buzzing all over her. Many of the men and women who went through such torture can identify with these forms of torture that also included rape as Otieno (1997) has discussed in her book.

The specific women's roles in the Mau Mau Movement included the following:

1.   Religious—The women were delegated to perform prayers for the Movement (traditional prayers mixed with Christian prayers as had been established then through the Independent Pentecostal Church). In almost all the battalions that were in various parts of either the Nyanda-

rua or the Mt. Kenya forest areas, there was a woman (women) who conducted this role, which sometimes included reading the signs and advising the troops of the ensuing dangers. This role of "mundu-mugo" (customary foreseer) or "prophet" was well respected and honored, as in most cases it served to avert what would have been dangerous situations leading to loss of lives if the foreseer's advice and guidance was not followed.

2. Spying/Intelligence Gathering—The women were recruited and swore oaths to be loyal to the Movement, and specifically to collecting intelligence which would help the troops in the Land Freedom Army (the Mau Mau military wing). They were expected to use their persuasive mannerisms to intelligently gather any useful information from the enemies—mainly the colonial government and the loyalists (policemen, chiefs, home guards and others). Some would befriend the enemy, not because they cared for them but because they wanted to get information which they eventually passed to the Mau Mau organizers. They were good at gathering intelligence and were relied on both in the Reserve and also in the forests.

3. Collecting Guns and Other War Items—The women were in many instances charged with the duty of ensuring a supply of weapons, especially guns. This role was closely linked to the spying one above. In the course of befriending the administration soldiers or the home guards, the women were expected to calculate the best time for them to sneak away with the guns the soldiers had. It was not by use of force but cunning that would eventually produce guns, bullets and other war related materials that the Mau Mau most needed. Ideally they had to act in a way that these armed men fell for them and would not openly realize the motive of the women. Given the assumption that the women were not seen as a threat to these armed men, they were able to take advantage of them and certainly "stole" weapons from them that were of much benefit to the Movement.

4. Transporting Goods to the Forest—The women, more than the men, were the main conduit between the forest and the Reserve. Once foods, guns, bullets and medicine were gathered—either in Nairobi or in the various Reserves—the women were expected to disguise themselves as if they were going to their "shambas" (small farms) to cultivate. While acting as if they were going to their farms, they would transport needed valuables to the Mau Mau army. They could also carry some valuables in disguises that were not easily detected by the government; for example, they might pose as if pregnant in order to carry a number of valuables in what may be loosely referred to as the "front pouch." They were indeed a lifeline between the forest and the Reserves.

5. Combat—Women did not simply perform their traditional gender roles in this Movement. There are many oral and written facts showing that the women were involved in combat. They learned in the forest how to use guns and would do that when they were fighting against the enemy. They were not just cooking for the men or acting as "comfort ladies" but they were also in actual combat with the enemy.

6. "De Facto Heads of Households"—It was during the period of the Mau Mau Movement that many Kikuyu women, for example, became de facto heads of households. With their husbands gone for an indefinite period somebody had to step in to make household decisions that were previously the reserve of the male head of household. In the Kikuyu Reserve, this became the trend as many men had joined the Mau Mau military wing or were later imprisoned, and for that time (almost a decade) new gender relations were in formation, the women becoming more assertive and more comfortable with making major decisions about their children, their livestock and their farms. The women in the Reserve became the new custodians of property and children in the absence of their husbands.

7. Casual Laborers—The women were overburdened by not only being the heads of their households as noted above but also by being the main breadwinners for the period that their men were away. They became the engine of the local economy, mostly against their self will, and had to work for long hours and with little pay. They did not get enough time to attend their small farms, and this may explain why poverty and famine abound most of Central Province in the 1950s. They had little time to attend to their crops as they were forced to work for the loyalists albeit for next to nothing payment. Later in the 1950s, communal labor was introduced which required every household to participate in digging trenches (to protect soil erosion) or to literally dig for new roads in the Reserves. Such roads that were dug by the village communal labor led to the chief's compounds or their private farms. To this day (2005) I can identify such roads which were dug and leveled by women and children and the few men who had remained behind in the Reserves. One in my home area literally led to the local chief's farm.

Given that most of the men were either in the forest or detained in prison, the bulk of such forced labor was left to women and children. Many do not like remembering the harassment they endured during this period. Besides the harsh conditions of the communal labor that the women who remained behind in the Reserve faced, there were other forms of harassment targeted to the women. Humiliation by the home guards, the headmen and other loyalists was almost a daily event. This included both physical and verbal abuse, indiscriminate rape incidents as well as forceful abductions and pre-arranged marriages against the young woman's wishes. This was usually done as a way of buying protection from the home guards, the headmen or the chiefs. It is not a wonder then that almost all headmen, the chiefs and most home guards were scandalously polygamous, not so much for the reason that they were well endowed with possessions but much more for the power they wielded. Girl children were married off to the powerful in order to ensure safety of a particular family from the colonial rule and possibilities of one being sent to prison or one's material goods being forcefully taken by the loyalists. Some of these forced marriages ended in separation after independence as they were marriages of convenience. A good number of the women who had been forced by their relatives or parents into such arrangements could not take it any more after independence when the loyalists' power to coerce and hassle was no more. They walked away from those polygamous homes that were never in the first place their dream of a good marriage or home!

Women's contributions to the Mau Mau Movement directly and indirectly have to be acknowledged as they were a reality. It is a shame that just like their fellow poor, landless members of the Movement, they also did not benefit much after independence. The Movement was hijacked by the "landed" Kikuyu, the new elites (political and economic), especially the sons of the loyalists who had oppressed them during the times of struggle. Without the women's contributions as outlined above, the Mau Mau military wing, which fought strongly and consistently for four consecutive years (1952-1956) until their leader Dedan Kimathi was arrested, would have been weakened in the first or the second year. Any army has to be fed, otherwise its performance will be dismal. It was the women who maintained that lifeline and when it was really weakened in the late 1950s, the Mau Mau armies in the forest felt the blow. The kind of hunger described in the narrative that follows came when the lifeline between the Reserve and the forests was dramatically curtailed by having many more aggressive colonial soldiers in the Reserve and the "Kwa Mwanya" (no man's land areas). The communal labor that was introduced and the curfew were the administration's tactful way to ensure that they could account for all the women in the Reserve. It was a way of ensuring that their active role of transporting and spying, for example, was dealt a blow. It was a war strategy aimed at an overall weakening of the Mau Mau Movement. When the women were targeted, the administration was able to achieve their goals of weakening the Movement.

In the following chapters (4-12) I will shift to the praxis section of this book, which is mainly a narration of a non-fiction story as told by a participant of the Mau Mau Movement from the mobilization stages to the fighting in the forest. This narration was written originally in the Kikuyu language. I have translated it and left it pretty much as it was in the original language. I will summarize and conclude the book in Chapter 14.

Chapter 4

The Beginnings

It was early morning of October 28, 1952, when we awoke at Kiamwangi Junior Secondary School, a boarding school. We hauled out of the dormitory, initially by the loud noises of many vehicles, which were arriving in many numbers at the school compound as early as between six and seven in the morning. From nine in the morning, our school compound was full of policemen and soldiers, who after a short while ordered all the students to huddle up in groups belonging to one's district of origin.

There were students from almost all districts of Kenya represented in Kiamwangi: some were from the Coast Province, others from the Rift Valley, still others from Nyanza, Kitui District, Nyeri, Murang'a, Embu, Meru, Machakos and Kiambu. Indeed there were very few parts of Kenya that may not have been represented in Kiamwangi. In those days, both young and old were going to school—even married men, like one relatively older man who was my friend, called Nathan Kariuki Gakuru. He was married with one child. The idea that was predominant then was for everybody to acquire education, at least to know how to read and write, so that when we started to fight for our independence, people would be aware as to what we were fighting for!

What that meant is that education was seen as the medium to get into people's brains and with education, this would facilitate easier communication. Our people would be able to read newspapers for themselves and would get the idea of what was going on; they would also be able to read their own letters, and this would give them a sense of what independence and freedom from colonialism was all about. They would know the meaning of "wiyathi" (freedom). Most of our people at this time were indeed anxious to learn how to read and write. Fortunately, around this time (in the early 1950s) there was a sizable African contingent of relatively educated men who were willing to teach the others and share the new Western education. This heightened the demand for education for most of the young men. A number of young men not only learned the basic education but some progressed to some of the prominent schools of those days like Alliance High School, Kagumo High School, Kabaa High School, Maseno High School and others. Others who passed well in their high school exams were admitted at Makerere University, which was then the only university (for Kenya, Uganda and Tanganyika) and it was then called the University of East Africa until 1970 when Kenya established the University of Nairobi and Tanganyika established the University of Dar-es-Salaam.

In those days when we were going to school, I was filled with a lot of desire to acquire as much education as I possibly could. I was always dreaming and wishing to become as educated as one of our teachers, whose name was John Gitau whom I heard had come from Makerere University. I felt with my whole heart that I would also at one time end up being a Makerere student, whatever it took!

I believe because of my strong desire to go to Makerere, I was enjoying my education and I was becoming very good at it. Whenever Mr. Gitau asked a question in class, I was always ready to answer it. It was myself and another young man called Kagombe who were always ready to answer the teacher's questions. Because of our seriousness and hardworking habits, Mr. Gitau liked us a lot. The principal of Kiamwangi School, the late Mr. Stephen J. Kioni also liked the two of us very much because we were good students. Because of the happy atmosphere that was in the school among both teachers and students, the academic performance in this school was excellent and teachers frequently visited us from other schools in the country eager to see for themselves the bright students and the famous school.

As the fame of the school spread nationwide, the principal of one of the best government schools, Alliance High School, an Englishman whose name was E. Carey Francis, visited us. He came to visit our school on March 22, 1951. When he came to our school, Mr. Kioni accompanied by Mr. Gitau took him around all the classrooms from Standard VI to Form III. He was also taken around the dormitories and he learned that from Standard VI to Form III, there were 1,301 students that included young men, young women as well as relatively older men who were all very thirsty for the Western education, especially eager to learn how to read and write.

The visiting Englishman realized truly that the Africans were really longing for more education, especially those who were already in our school. However, he also knew that he would not be able to take all of them to Alliance (his good school) as they would not fit—they were just too many! He instructed Mr. Kioni and Mr. Gitau to select the brightest students and he arranged with them a situation where every year, he would admit one of the brightest students from Kiamwangi to Alliance High School as a way of helping our school. This is exactly what was done and that very year, our two teachers chose Kagombe as the one designated to attend Alliance the following year and, indeed, in January 1952, Kagombe went to Alliance.

On the second selection, I was the one selected, and I was to go to Alliance in January 1953. Indeed a letter of admission to Alliance was sent in my name so that I could know well in advance and get ready to report to Alliance the following year where I had secured a seat. I do not want to say that this is why I did not go to Alliance High School, but suffice it to say that after I got the news of my selection, I was full of pride, and I was boasting to the other students that I was not as thick as they were! I also used to abuse them and tell them that when I go to Makerere University and come back, I will be employing some of them to work as my laborers on my farm because their heads were full of worms instead of brains and that is why they were thick in class and were doing poorly academically.

I was extremely proud and then Mr. Gitau loved me so much that I was given a nickname of praise, which meant "the heart of the class"—I was really feeling like I was on top of the world! I would also on many occasions accompany Mr. Gitau for visits to his home area of Kahuguini. Keeping the company of a teacher those days was like the greatest achievement and this made me more proud that I can possibly explain by mere words. I was as proud as a peacock! I could not explain to myself why I was feeling that proud. I was also full of happiness knowing that the following year I was going to Alliance High School. It made me feel like I was the brightest person that ever lived! I remember some mathematics problems called "compound proportion" that Mr. Gitau used to show me from a book written by E. Carey Francis, and he would tell me that when I go to Alliance, I would be exposed to them more. That is because I would be taught by the famous mathematician of the times who taught at Alliance High School. There were other math problems called "algebra" which Mr. Gitau told me I will get more exposed to when I went to Makerere.

I really believed in myself that I would at one time get into Makerere, and I think anyone seeing that kind of fortune was bound to feel as proud as I was feeling. I was thinking of the fact that we were so many in our school and it was only Kagombe and myself who were bright enough to be admitted to Alliance. "If only wishes were horses!" As it turned out my wishful thinking all came to naught. There are times I felt like blaming God for my misfortune, especially for not achieving my education goals, but then as I think more and evaluate my life; I feel He has done so much more for me than attaining the education goals. Indeed the good God has guided me and saved me in worse and hostile situations, and it was not because of my own ability or academic knowledge like the kind I would have gotten in Makerere. He has just guided me and loved me for whom I am and here I would say, "Praise the Lord!" He is the giver of life and the Almighty! Indeed even after all the pride I showed to everybody, none of those things I was being proud of was ever achieved---I never went to Alliance High School, I never went to Makerere. I cannot even show you where their gates were. I do not know whether their gates face North or South, which color they are, black or white. It is only God who knows the reasons, for today I would be Dr. So-and-So or Professor So-and-So, but none of this came to fruition! This tends to confirm the Kikuyu saying that, "muugi ndoi uria akerwo" ("he who knows does not know what he will be told") and another one that says "Iciaraga uuru mwene amiroreire" ("a cow or a goat will have birth complications when the owner is right there watching it") and finally "uuge wa Ngai nduri mugaruri na iri kuhitia na migwi ndirathaga na njoya" ("God's word has no challenge and when it misses with the arrow, it won't pierce with the feathers").

There is however another Kikuyu saying, "itihitagia thome wa cio (ii indo)," that is, if one family household was well endowed with riches either of wealth from having many farm animals like goats, even if all of them were stricken by a serious disease and they all died, at one time in the future that household will one day get new and many goats. It is similar to the other Kikuyu proverb which says that "gutiri nyumba iri kahii itakarugwo mutwe" (that is, any household that has a male child will at one time have a goat's head cooked and eaten by the family members). We should note that the goat was/is a delicacy among the Kikuyu and while the poor may not afford a goat, this saying implies that it is not futile to expect a turnaround of poverty, especially in a home where a male child was born. Indeed the lesson from all this is to have faith in God as no one really can predict the facts of the future.

Chapter 5

The Beginning of Trials and Tribulations

That early morning of November 28, 1952, will always be in my memories because that is when I got the misfortune of missing my aspired education achievements. From that time I have come to realize the helplessness of the human being in deciding on their future. It is God's plan that the human beings try to fit in!

After being commanded by an African soldier, who had the rank of a corporal, that we all sit together in groups according to our districts of origin, we did exactly that without any knowledge as to why we were doing it. We were simply following the orders. Slightly after nine in the morning, a police vehicle came to our school compound carrying six white policemen, all of them in the ranks of "Inspector." They were immaculately dressed in their well-shined police uniform. When they arrived, they were shown where they could sit, a place that had been prepared outside for this purpose. All the six sat on the prepared platform. The soldiers sat behind the students and the teachers, surrounding us. Only Mr. Kioni, the principal, was allowed to sit in the front with the white policemen. Mr. Gitau at this time was not at the school as he had gone back to Uganda, at his Makerere University to finish up his studies.

When the white policemen were finally seated, one of them who had a long and thick mustache did not sit down; he immediately stood on the platform ready to address us. He was highly decorated with stars on his shoulder lapels and on his chest. His presence and mean look was enough to demand obedience and nobody would dare look directly into his eyes as he was profoundly intimidating, especially to the Africans. His shining stars and medals symbolized his senior position in the Forces which suggested that whatever he said was followed strictly as if it was the law without anyone raising an objection. If he ordered that we all be shot, that is exactly what would have happened as all the soldiers and the policemen who surrounded us were heavily armed with guns.

He did not waste any time at all and within a few seconds, he had stepped up on the platform and he started talking in English very courageously and with a lot of confidence. He was straight and firm as he delivered his speech and he appeared like he had been planted where he stood and like that was his spot from when he was born. With a sharp and a firm commanding voice, he announced the following: "From today, the 28th of November 1952, this school has been closed and all other Independent Schools like this one anywhere in the country. The government of O.H.M.S (On her Majesty's Service) Her Majesty Queen Elizabeth has learned that these schools have been the location where the Mau Mau oath has been administered and therefore from today those schools will never ever be operated as institutions of learning. They will be closed for good by the government! Among you, there are some that have taken the Mau Mau oath and I will call their names aloud. Once I call them they should stand up and the police will accompany them to the waiting vehicles and they will give the details of their participation in the oath at the police station.

"Those of you whom I will not call your names aloud should remain just the way you are seated. You will all be taken to your respective homes. You should then be careful not to sit amongst people who are not from your district. Besides, as from this moment, none of you should go back to your classes or your dormitories as there is a likelihood that those who have taken the oath might run away and the government is really interested in interrogating them. You should therefore just sit still wherever you are and very soon names of all of you will be called aloud and as soon as you are called you will be expected to jump onto one of the vehicles that you see here that will take you back to your rural home. Be sure not to enter a vehicle that is not arranged to go to your home district!"

Up to this time, we did not know the purpose of the vehicles that had started coming to our school as early as 6:00 a.m., and all of them being packed in the school field. But when we heard that names would be called aloud and we should enter the vehicles as we were called, then we knew the purpose of the vehicles and that they were the ones which would take us home.

During the period that we were in that school, we used to get frequent visits from leaders of other Independent Schools from various regions that had these kind of schools. Many seniors Africans who knew the importance of the Mau Mau oath also visited us. We were also visited by the leaders of the political party called K.A.U. (Kenya African Union) like Jomo Kenyatta, Mbiyu Koinange, Eliud Mathu, Dedan Mugo, Solomon Memia and other African senior personalities in our country at that time. We also got visitors from as far as South Africa, especially one that was called Professor Bellington Mamphele.

Those elders had written some songs, which were sung by the students in the school, although not many of the students could tell the real significance of those songs. One of the songs was as follows:

Andu aitu, ukirai, tuingate thina, tuingate
Thina, tuingate thina uyu, Ni urimu na ukigu (x 2)
Tuingate thina uyu (x 3)

[Our people wake up, we have to chase poverty away, chase poverty away, it is foolishness and stupidity (x 2), we chase this poverty away (x 3)]

And another one goes like this:

Gikuyu thimo kuingiha, wega umaga mucii
Kahiu kogi inoro thome, College ni inorero,
Njamba ciitu (x 3), iromama kuuraga

[The Kikuyu have many proverbs, "Righteousness starts at ones own home," "a sharp knife has to have a file at the entrance," "the college is the place to sharpen the brains," "our great leaders (x 3), should escape from death."]

Even though most of the songs we sang at school did not make sense at that time, later on they all made sense, for we witnessed many of the things we sang about as we went on with life. Indeed most of the things came to be seen in the country gradually. I may not write all those songs here, but I will highlight just a few more:

Aciari mutuhe turamu, mbara yoka tukoimaimira tutangire njamba ciitu cia Gikuyu, wathi wakura wendaga uungi.

[Parents, give us pens, when the war comes, we will come to the front and guard the leaders of the Gikuyu people, as a generation grows old, it should be succeeded by a younger one.]

Andu oothe ngundu tungatirai, ciana ciothe nacio ciuhige, ni amu mahinda maria me matuku maya, mbaara yao no ya karamu.

[All of us should protect our land, all the children should be educated, because the times we are in, the only weapon to fight the war is the pen.]

Bata wa itimu ni muthiru, riu utigaire wa karamu, ni amu mahinda maria me matuku maya mbaara yao no ya karamu.

[The importance of the spear is long gone, what is remaining now is the importance of the pen, because at this time the only weapon to fight the war is the pen.]

And another one that was sung as follows:

Wengenge uyu muingi wa Gikuyu, Mburi na ngombe ni ciathirire, maga guthoma no makoimira, githi to gutwika njika kamba.

[The young children of the Gikuyu, goats and cattle are long gone, if you do not go to school, you will not make it anywhere but you will remain retrogressive.]

Mugunda mwega uri Githunguri, handu hakuhi na barabara, uri ituamba ing'etheirie Kirinyaga, ni mwega wa guturwo ni ciana.

[The beautiful garden is in Githunguri, somewhere near the road, it has beautiful plains facing Mt. Kenya, it is so beautiful that the children could live there forever.]

Githunguri was the Teacher Training College as well as a school that was the premier of the Independent Schools where Jomo Kenyatta and Mbiyu Koinange (its founder) once taught. This is why it is described as an equivalent of the Garden of Eden for the young children who were thirsty for education.

Within no time, the names were called aloud and those called headed straight to the vehicles that were designated to take them to their home districts. The first group to be called was those who hailed from the Rift Valley, followed by those from Kitui, Coast Province, then Kisumu (Nyanza Province), then Nyeri, and then Murang'a, my home district. After that I do not know who followed because no sooner than had our groups been all called, the doors were shut and two policemen who had the list with all our names joined us. The bossy white policeman instructed them that they should ensure that all of us were taken each to their home area.

That is exactly what was done and two vehicles left at the same time headed for Murang'a. I think Murang'a had the most students in the school, although I am not very certain about this given that I did not witness all the student groups from all the other districts since we had to leave before the whole operation was over.

We started our journey for Murang'a district at around ten in the morning, headed for Thika. At Thika, we were divided into two groups: one vehicle carried those who came from two adjacent divisions. Ours carried those from Kandara and Kigumo division, and the other carried those from Kangima and Kiharu divisions.

We asked the policemen who were guarding us whether we could buy some food at Thika because we were hungry especially because we had not had breakfast that morning. They were kind enough, and they did not refuse. We bought snacks like bread (mandazi) and then we were urged to get back to the vehicles and eat in there as we continued with our journey. Our vehicle started off headed for Gatanga. When the vehicle got near to the home of one of us, we were expected to inform the policeman so that the vehicle could stop. The idea was for the policeman to be able to identify a relative of the student, the parent, the chief or the headman of the village who would be responsible enough to ensure that the student had reached home safely. Along the way, students were dropped off as each got near their homes until we got to our place, where six of us were to alight. When we got to our shopping center, we found many of our neighbors who were taken by surprise when they saw us being escorted home by the policemen and strange vehicles. When we said that this was our place, the policeman asked the people there whether they knew us and almost all of them answered in the affirmative that they knew us well! When we alighted from the vehicle, those still remaining were taken to their respective homes. We were later communicating through letters finding out how it all went with them. Later on we learned that everyone was taken to their homes safely.

When we were finally left alone with the people from our home area, they were curious and they wanted to hear from us what was happening and why we were brought home by the police from our school. Since we did not have much details ourselves as to what was really happening, we only told them what the bully white policeman had told us that, "all the Independent Schools had been closed forthwith and they will never ever be opened again." Those people did not show much worry, but I think it is mainly because they were already aware of the fact that the Africans were demanding their independence and freedom. They had also taken the Mau Mau oath, which I only came to learn a bit later when we got to interact more with them, as I will explain below.

At our shopping center, as soon as the vehicle that had brought us left, the people bought us food and drinks as we were hungry having not had a proper meal for the whole day, from the time the saga started at school. When we got full, we started walking towards our homes independently. I was accompanied by another young man whose name was Muchiri, as we were immediate neighbors. When we got home, we found my sister and my other siblings. My parents were not there, and when I inquired where they were, I was told they had gone to visit another village elder, whose name was Mwaniki.

My sister got busy to ensure that we got something to eat since it was getting dark and she thought we were hungry. She made food for us and for the other children. She was showing a lot of love and happiness to us, but I could also tell she was a little bit worried because she had been hearing about the Mau Mau. Since she was still young, she did not understand fully what it was all about and what was really going on. At that time, the only thing one heard about the Mau Mau was the negative propaganda that was propagated by the colonial government. The government propaganda was that Mau Mau was an evil organization, which has a membership of gangsters and killers and much more negative stuff.

After our meal it was late, and I asked Muchiri to spend the night at my place and the following day we could go to his place. That is just what we did. We kept waiting for my parents to come back, but they never came back that night. They came back the following morning. When they came back the following morning, I was suspicious that they probably had gone to take the Mau Mau oath or they had gone to administer it to others. Since I could not ask them directly, I just kept quiet with my own suspicions.

I went with Muchiri the following day to his place and when we got there, we found that his parents were also not at home. When he inquired where they were, he was told that they had left the previous night and they had not come back. Since I was getting rather agitated about the quietly talked Mau Mau oath, I requested Muchiri to let me leave for home so as to monitor more what was going on. We agreed that if he found anything about it he could let me know and the vice-versa for me. We had to keep each other posted on whatever we were able to gather concerning this oath! When I got back home, I found my father had come back all right, but because of the general uneasiness that was on the land, one could tell that he was not very happy. We talked quite much that evening and he inquired about school and I told him a lot of what he wanted to know.

The following morning, at around 11 o'clock, three people that I did not know came to our home compound. They had long hair, which was covered with hats. They also had long beards. They called my father on the side near a shade for a tête-à-tête. I could not hear what they were telling him in their low tones, and I could not ask my father for after their discussion, my father accompanied them and they left. My father did not come back home until the following morning. When my father came back, I tried to find out from him who those people were but he did not disclose who they were. That night, we heard gunfire near our village shopping center, but we did not know why. Around 11 o'clock the following morning, an elder of the area whose name was Gerishon, came to our place and found me with my father seated at a corner of the compound. He told my father, "Son of Wanjiru, which direction should we take since this place has become very insecure?" My father asked him immediately to explain what had gone wrong! He told my father that the previous night when we were running after hearing the gun shots, one of the neighbors was shot and died from those gun shots. The neighbor's name was Gitau. Gitau was shot last night!

I could tell that the two old men were really worried and saddened by this news. They just woke up and headed towards the village shopping center so as to find more details about Gitau's death. When they came back in the evening, they were just talking about the Gitau incident. They had learned that he was shot while on his way back home from the shopping center where he had gone to buy some goods that he had been requested to do by the Mau Mau. The items included medicine, matchboxes and cigarettes, which he still was in possession of at the time he was shot.

After two days, the chief called for a meeting and he ordered that it was a mandatory meeting and everyone should attend it without failure. Anyone who would miss the meeting would be accountable to show where the Mau Mau people were hiding. The chief practically knew all the villagers and their homes and so it was easy for him to identify any absentee. He also announced that the district officer would be there to address the meeting and he also would like everybody from the area to be present at the meeting. Due to the grief that had stricken everybody in the area as a result of Gitau's death from the gunshots, nobody failed to turn up at the meeting. Everyone feared they might be next hence the huge turnout.

Once the people gathered, the district officer (D.O.), the chief and the sub-chief came and found people sitting down. The askaris (administration police) as well the home guards were standing as if they were guarding the seated crowd. As soon the D.O. arrived, he shot out of his car with a piece of paper on which eighteen names were written. Those names were reportedly of the Mau Mau in the area.

After holding a short brief with the chief, the D.O. started calling out the names of the eighteen persons. When he was done, he asked those he called to get into his vehicle. He also ordered the askaris and the home guards to keep an eye on them to ensure they did not run away because they were the worst Mau Mau! Thereafter, the D.O. started talking to the rest of the crowd. He was addressing the people in English and the chief was doing the translation. He was talking with a lot of anger and he told the people at the meeting that he had already known that the village had a lot of Mau Mau. He suggested that all those who were in that meeting and belonged to the Mau Mau should stand and voluntarily give themselves up to the authorities before he called out their names like the eighteen he had just called out. Whoever didn't come forward voluntarily and belonged to the evil movement (Mau Mau) would be punished thoroughly once identified.

Everybody kept quiet and people were just looking at each other without saying a thing to each other, filled with fear and anxiety. After a short while, the D.O. became so mad and he said to the people, "since you have refused to turn yourselves in voluntarily, I order you now to leave and walk to your homes without anyone looking behind. Whomever turns to look behind will be shot dead immediately without any questions asked!"

That is exactly what people did; everyone walked away towards their homes without a single one turning back because they knew the D.O. was dead serious and they would be shot had they turned to check what was behind them. Before everyone dispersed from the shopping area, they heard gun shots, but, because of fear, no one dared to turn their heads. The gun shots continued for some time. Most of us then thought that the eighteen people we left behind were being shot.

When we got to our homes, people gathered in the night so as to seek ways and means to get over the problem of insecurity in the area. They feared that if the situation of indiscriminate arrests continued, then the government would come to know the secrets of the Mau Mau, especially the oathing. The people were concerned that if the government got to know that almost everybody in the area had taken the Mau Mau oath, then we would all be arrested and possibly killed.

After a lot of discussions and sharing of opinions, a general consensus was reached that the best place to run away from the colonial government was in the forest. It was agreed upon to establish a criterion to choose those who would go to the forest. It was also agreed upon that those who would go to the forest would be given another oath of the battle (the platoon oath) which would instill in them more confidence and courage to fight against the brutal colonial government. That oath was prepared and most of the young men and the older men who were not too old (in their thirties and forties) were chosen to take the oath which was called "muma wa mbatuni," or the "platoon oath."

That whole issue (the oath and the criterion to choose) was well handled by the leaders and it was agreed that 180 young men would be chosen to go to the forest and start fighting against the colonial government. They were to start as soon as possible before the colonial government got wind of the preparations that were underway. It was an urgent matter given that they feared that the government might get to know about their plans before they actually implemented them. Also a number of things had to be prepared in advance: (1) identifying where guns and bullets would come from; (2) identifying where clothes and food would be coming from; (3) identifying where medicine and clinicians would come from; and (4) identifying service assistants in the Gikuyu Reserve who would be coordinating with the fighters to ensure supply of goods needed as well as information about the enemy. These were an important link with the forest fighters as they were responsible for keeping everything ready to ensure efficiency when those from the forest came to take the goods from the Reserve.

All plans were carried out without a hitch, mainly because all the people were cooperative and were talking in unity hence there were no disagreements. All the people had sworn when they took the Mau Mau oath that among other things which I will not write in details here, they were ready to fight at all costs until they got "Uhura" (independence). Now, Kenya is independent and this is really what was in everybody's mind when the plans to go to the forest were being arranged. Independence was not just a demand for the Gikuyu who were preparing to go to the forest, but all the people of Kenya were demanding it.

Chapter 6

Getting into the Forest

It was on March 20, 1953, and I was sitting outside our home compound under a "mukoe" tree when a young man by the name Gedraph came towards me running and looking very worried. He was also thoroughly beaten and you could see whip marks all over his body. His upper lip was swollen and was as big as a "gitaruru" (traditional mat), and it was covering his mouth. You could not tell where a lip covered his mouth used to be, as it was appearing like it that I couldn't possibly explain how it was.

When he reached where I was seated, he asked me, "'Thiari' (my friend), how come you are just seated here relaxed? Don't you know how our people have been killed and others shot and are now cripples and you are just sitting here where the home guards will find you and do the same to you?" I tried to ask him what was going on but he did not want to spend time talking out there as he feared the home guards might arrive any time and continue with the beating and maiming or killing that they had already started on him. He told me that if I wanted to spare my life, I should follow him and go to the forest and he would tell me all that was going on. He said he himself was then headed for the forest and indeed he did not wait for my full reply as he just took off running towards the slopes of the Kayuyu River, and I saw him climb the hill on the opposite side headed towards the Aberdares (Nyandarua) forest.

I was left there mesmerized and shocked not knowing whether to follow him or which direction I would take mainly because the timetable that had been set for going to the forest was not yet due hence my confusion. On that evening, news spread detailing how bad it had become and how our people were being tortured by the government agents. It was decided that all the young men who had been chosen as the ones who would go to the forest should meet immediately in one of the homes of the elders. The home that we were to meet belonged to a Mr. Njuguna, and it was mandatory that we all were there. That is exactly what we did, and at ten o'clock in the night we all met at Njuguna's.

When we got there, we found everything had been properly arranged. It was decided that we were not going to wait any longer because it was feared that the longer we waited the more likelihood that the government would know about our plans and we would all be arrested, and if that happened there would be nobody to go to the forest. Immediately after arrival at Njuguna's, those who had not taken the "platoon oath" had to take it right away, and all the usual ceremonies associated with the oath were administered that very night. While we were just sitting there eating and talking, those people who had been assigned the duty of guarding the compound that we were in against possible enemy infiltration came at around seven o'clock in the morning and told us that the army of the Kings African Rifles (KAR) as well as the police and the home guards were coming headed to the compound where we were. They suspected someone might have gone out to betray us and the meeting we were holding at Njuguna's. They suggested that the best solution, then, was for all of us to head directly to the forest because if we were to be found there, we would all are eliminated. During the period we were at Njuguna's, I noticed that there were some people, around forty of them, that I did not know and they were all wearing overcoats. Some had guns, which for me was the first time to see a gun at a close range. I heard that the new people I could not recognize had come from Nairobi.

When one of those forty men heard that the police and the army were headed our way, he said "Let them come, we will wage a battle right here!" The elder men, who were also the local leaders, advised that it was not good to have a battle right there with the government agents because it would be very tough for those who remained behind after the young men go to the forest. They feared that the government would indiscriminately torture the elderly, the women and the children of that general neighborhood who would be accused of having assisted the Mau Mau. If they were all killed, this would not be good as they were the ones who would be assisting those who went to the forest, especially making arrangements for their food supplies. Those forty men agreed, and there was a general consensus not to fight right there as the elders had advised.

After the resolution to go to the forest, we all went headed for Nyandarua filled with happiness, especially when we noted that we were in the company of people who had guns. We felt protected! Because of all the preaching that had been done to us about the importance of Uhura and getting back our stolen lands from the colonial settlers, we felt strong enough to fight any battle that came our way without any fear.

We went up along Gita-biki River and we entered the Nyandarua forest in a big group of 240 men and women. We had five women in our group. When we got into the forest, at the place that we first settled, we found other people, approximately 300, whom we had no idea that they were already in the forest. When they saw us, they were very happy because they had been waiting for us. Our leaders had informed them that we were on the way.

Although it appears like I am narrating a story, it is very sad for anyone who has the memories of the period I am writing about. However given that many people just heard about this period of time I will narrate the "story" so that they can learn and know that the Uhuru (independence) that we have now came from quite a distance and that we struggled for it. It was NOT given to us on a platter!

When we arrived at that camp, we found one captain whose name was Capt. Njatha. He welcomed us with much happiness, and he introduced us to all his soldiers as well as showing us all the guns that were in their possession. They had many kinds of guns like machine guns, rifles and "gotora," automatic guns. They also were in possession of hand grenades! At that time I came to learn that among the people who had guns whom we entered the forest with, one of them was the famous and highly respected General Kago, another one was Captain Muiruri. I learned who they were from the way Captain Njatha was greeting them, with a lot of respect and calling them by their names and titles. I also learned that the camp at which we found Cap. Njatha was called Ndiara Bush.

After staying at that Camp for one week, General Kago wanted to have all those who had come from Location 1 to move there because at that time the home guards and the soldiers were really hard on the people of Location 1. The people there were under strict surveillance from the government army and others were being arrested indiscriminately and detained without any trials and without explanation offered.

General Kago said his goodbyes to Captain Njatha as well as the other people from Location 2. As you probably may guess, the goodbyes involved a renewed commitment and promise to each other to keep fighting hard until they chased the white colonial government off the Africans' backs!

After saying the goodbyes, we started the journey headed for Location 1 right within the forest. We set off at about two o'clock in the afternoon. That journey was rather taxing because we had carried food like maize, sweet potatoes and plantains. The maize was the greatest amount of the food we carried which indeed was what was expected and planned for because, hard maize takes long before rotting as would some of the other more fragile food like plantains. Each person carried at least 60 to 80 pounds of maize, depending on one's ability.

After trekking for quite a long while, it became dark and, given that everybody was tired, General Kago told us that we would not move any further. He advised us that we build a small camp to spend just that night so as to be strong enough to continue with the journey the following day until we met the other group in Location 1. When we were told that we would go until we met the other people, we were surprised because up to then we thought we were the only ones in the forest as well as Capt. Njatha's group which was in Location 2.

We built our small temporary camp quickly since there was lots of bamboo. It was also raining hard because it was around April, the long rainy season. We made our temporary beds; we cooked enough to eat that night and to carry for our lunch the following day. In the morning, we started our journey, and by three o'clock in the afternoon, we had arrived at our destination. When we arrived, we were met by other people who were very happy to receive us. They knew we were on our way, despite the fact that we did not know that we were meeting any people there. We found they had cooked a lot of food and a lot of meat which was enough to feed the 1,040 people who were there. I was very pleasantly surprised because I had no clue that what we were doing was as well planned as it now appeared. I was also happy to realize the purpose and goal of our being in the forest: mainly to fight the colonial white government and get our "Uhuru." I was filled with even more happiness when I looked around and was very impressed with the magnitude of our numbers. We were many! The men we found who were leading the group we found at the new location were a Mr. Mbugua and a Mr. Mwangi.

After eating and drinking, we started singing different kinds of songs like the following:

Ni ndotete na ngamenya nitukuhotana, tondu kihoto twinakio gitiri kirora.

[I have dreamt and I know we shall win this war, because our purpose and goals are clear and we have not lost the direction.]

CHORUS: Uui, thina ni muuru, uui thina ni muuru

Rugendo rwakwa rwa Ol Kalou nindagiririo thii ni Kamau na Mukuna, nio magiririe thii.

[My journey to Ol Kalou, I was not allowed to go by Kamau and Mukuna; they are the ones who refused me to go.]

Murata wakwa tiga kurira, ndacoka mutitu ningacoka tuine ruimbo turiganirie thina.

[My friend do no not cry, when I come back from the forest we will a song to drown our sorrows!]

And another one like this one:

Kiugo kia mbere na inyui anake, mutungatire bururi, mwathina thina nduriaga, thutha no inyui mukoimira.

[The first important thing for you young men, is to serve your country, if you are poor, poverty cannot consume a man, and in the end you will come out triumphantly!]

CHORUS: Ungiurio, atia! II nawe atia! "Kana uri Mugikuyu?" Ingioya moko meri na iguru, Njuge nii ndi Mugikuyu!

[CHORUS: If perchance you are asked, "Are you a Mugikuyu (a (Kikuyu)?" I would raise both of my hands up high and declare that I am truly a Mugikuyu (a Kikuyu)!]

Kiugo gia keri na inyui anake, munyitane na Athuri anyu, mutungatire muri hamwe muhote nyina Karwigi na ithe.

[The second important thing is for you young men to join hands with your Elders, that way you serve together and in unity and you will be able to defeat both Mother Hawk and Father Hawk!]

Tugitigana arata aitu, ni wega mumenye ati ni miiri iki yatigana na ngoro ikorwo iri hamwe.

[When we are parting, our friends, let's know clearly that it is only the bodies that are parting but our souls will still be together.]

And another one like this:

Arata thina wina arume, rekei tuminyue na John na Willy murata wa John tu-coke tumuhe gitumi.

[Friends, problems are always with men, let's drink together with John and Willy and thereafter we will give him the reason.]

Kwari hakuhi na miaraho tukiigua tugitwo tukiria, tukiirwo tukire na ihenya Willy agiukira na kaihuri.

[It was about lunchtime and we had someone calling us while we were eating. We were told to wake up quickly and Willy woke up with his calabash.]

Twagereirio kwa munene umwe, nake aari wa nyota ithatu, akiuria giki nikio kiama kiria gicaragia wiyathi?"

[We were taken to one of the leaders who were decorated and had three stars, he asked us whether this was the group that was fighting for independence.]

Twaragia twina uchamba muingi tondu wa kumenya gitumi, tukiirwo tweterere nginya macokio makoima Kwa anene.

[We were speaking with a lot of courage because we knew the reason for our fighting and being in the forest, we were then told to wait until the response came from the leaders.]

Njeri muiritu wa Kariara na Njoki muiritu wa Iyigo, nio acio mukuona mbica-ini magitungatira bururi.

[Njeri, a lady from Kariara, and Njoki a lady from Iyigo, they are the ones you can see here in the picture in the service of their country!]

Even without writing all the songs we sang, suffice it to say that each song had a particular time and moment when it was sung. Songs served a particular purpose and were a response to what was happening to us on a daily basis. They were a means of communication and recording of our memories.

We stayed at that camp which was called Makiama Bush for about four months with peace and with no enemy attack despite the fact that we knew the harassment our aides were getting in the Reserve. One morning, General Kago, our general, called everyone to attention. He told us in a clear voice, "All of you who are here know the reason as to why you came to the forest. So far none of you has really done what we came to do here–that is, fight the colonial government and its supporters. We have not done the job we came to do! From this moment henceforth, everyone should be ready because tomorrow, we will go and attack one of the white government's camps. Today, I suggest that everybody should pray to God so that he can be with us until tomorrow and guide us in our attack mission. We should also pray that He should support us and lead us into victory just like in our agreed covenant with Him that if we win, it is not us who have won but Him, our God, and if we lose, it is not us who will lose but Him, our God!"

Nobody knew where we would be going the following day or where we would attack except the General himself, and his aides. The reason for the secrecy and for the people not to be informed is that it was clear there were some cowards amongst us and it was feared that if they knew ahead of time which camp we were going to attack, they might become informers for the government as a way of saving themselves, which would lead to a major disaster for us and for our supporters in the Reserve. The fear that the cowards might surrender to the police or the home guards was real in our leader's minds and this is why there was secrecy. It was also feared that once they surrendered, the cowards might give details of our whereabouts in the forest making us an easy prey for our enemies! Hence, only the leaders knew where we would be going to attack and no one else would be told before the actual day of action.

Almost everybody was excited, and they couldn't wait for the next day. Tomorrow seemed so far given that most of the people were really feeling thirsty for an exchange in a battle to fulfill one's commitment for going to the forest. Indeed, for the whole night, people were just excited and singing with a lot of joy in preparation for the following day!

In the morning of the Big Day, we were divided into three groups. Each group had 300 people and each group was given its special assignment. The group that I ended up being in was charged with the duty of going to open up the jail gates so as to let free our supporters who had been jailed; the other group was charged with waging a direct battle with the prison wardens; the third group was assigned the duty of burning and breaking into the shops as well as taking all the goods in those shops that we may need while back in the forest. Such goods included maize flour, maize, clothes and any available money which we would later use for buying medicine, matches and cigarettes.

Each group did the best it could in its assignment. Indeed each of them worked very hard until it won especially the one that was fighting with the prison wardens. We able to fight these wardens and dispossessed them of sixty guns, rifles and stern guns as well as pistols, revolvers and hand grenades. We also took from them their blight torches, clothes, shoes and different kinds of medicine.

After finishing the assignment, each group was showing a lot of happiness. In the group that I had been assigned, for example, we were so happy because we were able to free all the prisoners within a matter of a few minutes. Once we had them all free, they actually joined hands with our people and this helped our victory much more. Some also helped with carrying the goods we had collected back to the forest. Others were instrumental in showing us the shortcut back to the Nyandarua forest before the government soldiers reorganized themselves and started to follow us.

The number of people in our group was more than 1,400, and we climbed our way up heading for Nyandarua Mountains. At about ten o'clock in the morning we were all watching down below where the colonial soldiers were by the slopes of South Kinagop. By then we were right near the top of the Aberdares Mountains. They were following us but that was all in vain as we were far ahead of them and there was no way they could have caught up with us. We did the entire necessary job at night because it was dangerous for us to operate during the day as there were soldiers all over and we risked being victimized by the many soldiers. We also did not have many guns to fight with them, for example during this raid that we had just staged, we only had twenty-one guns. The entire raid was done in the night and by ten o'clock in the morning we were up high in the mountain enjoying the view and looking down far to see the government soldiers trying to follow us.

We rested up there in the high mountains until around one o'clock in the afternoon, and we ate the food that we had and after that General Kago guided us leading to the place we had left our other people. We got there at about four o'clock in the afternoon. When the people whom we had left behind saw us and saw the many guns we now had, they were extremely happy because they knew we did not have that many guns when we left. They were really excited and were hugging us all over with joy. Immediately they saw us they started singing many songs of joy as well as praising our God. Some of those songs were like this one:

Ni ndotete na ngamenya nitukuhotana, tondu kihoto twinakio gitiri kirora.

[I have dreamt and it has been revealed to me that we shall win this war, since we still have a clear reason and goal and that is not lost from us.]

CHORUS: Uui thina ni muru, uui thina ni muru ki.

[CHORUS: Oh, poverty is bad, oh, poverty is really bad.]

Rugendo rwakwa rwa Karau (Ol Kalou) nindagiririo thii, ni Kamau mena Mukuna, nio magiririe thii.

[My journey to Ol Kalou, I was refused to go by Kamau and Mukuna; they are the ones who made sure I could not go.]

Ndoimiriire uthiu wa murata ngiona uri muthitu, ngiringwo ni tha cia muru wa Maitu, Wuui, thina ni muru ki.

[I suddenly came face to face with a friend and I found that he was saddened, and I was touched by the sympathies of my brother, oh, poverty is really bad.]

Murata wakwa tiga kurira, ndacoka mbaraini, ningacoka tuine rwimbo turiganirie thina.

[My friend do not cry, I am going back to the war but I will eventually come back and we will sing a song together to forget our problems and poverty.]

As was our custom, General Kago thanked us very much for the victory that we had achieved and he told us that we had to invade the colonial soldiers and their establishments again so that we could amass more guns that would help us in our battles. His grand idea was, if possible, each of us in his battalion would have his own gun. That would make us always feel ready for any battle that we may encounter.

We spent the night in our camp full of joy and happiness and the following day, we assembled at the place we met to say our prayers. After the prayers, General Kago selected forty young men who would have to go up to Nyeri so as to inform our Commander-in-Chief, Mr. Dedan Kimathi, about the good news of our victory in attacking the Naivasha prison and that we were able to forcibly acquire sixty guns and that we also freed our people who had been jailed for no reason at all. It was important that Mr. Kimathi knew of our acquisition so that he could decide how the guns would be distributed since there were some battalion groups that had no guns at all or had too few that were not enough.

When our young men (soldiers) went to see the Commander-in-Chief, they came back with the instructions that Mr. Kimathi had issued. He had directed that those guns be divided into three. Our group was to be left with thirty guns; fifteen guns were to be given to Captain Njatha's group and the remaining fifteen to be sent to General Mbaria Kaniu. That is exactly what was done.

We stayed in that camp for a long time and we did not face any danger during that time. We only had disturbances from the planes flying over us but they did not injure with bombs any of our people. One early morning, General Kago called us where we normally gathered. He asked us to stay ready as we might be asked any time to go and invade one of the villages which he did not disclose at that time. He told us to be brave and courageous since where we would go would involve a big battle. Since we had given our souls for life or death, we did not fear anything and indeed we were eagerly looking forward to the day that we would be asked to go and attack.

After three days, we left the camp at eight o'clock in the evening, and our General told us that we were going to Njabi-ini, which is South Kinagop. We were 160 persons. We went very fast for we had reached our destination by one o'clock in the night. When we got near to where we were going to attack, General Kago arranged us in two groups in the order that we would carry out the invasion. I was in the group that was to do the slaughtering of the sheep that was being guarded by some policemen. Next to where the policemen were staying there were four houses, and there were also two planes, which belonged to the white settler who owned the sheep we were targeting for slaughter. That farm belonged to a white settler farmer whose name was Lee.

The other group was instructed to be the ones in the forefront fighting with the policemen. Those policemen were so lucky that none of them was shot dead. This was because when our troops started attacking, the policemen were sleeping in a different house from the one they invaded. The policemen were therefore able to exit from the house they were sleeping. When they heard the gunshots pointed to the other house, they knew they were being attacked and they ran away quietly hiding besides the other houses and they ran away without firing even a single shot. We, after some time, heard them shooting their guns from quite a distance.

When we heard their gun shots, we knew they had run away and since there is nothing we could have done at that time to get them, we felt disappointed since one of the things we really wanted was their guns. Now that they had run away, we just gave up on the guns. We searched their houses thoroughly looking for anything that would be of interest to us. We found three boxes full of bullets, their shoes, their sweaters, cooking pots, plates and cups, and we made sure that we carried everything since we needed them as much. By that time, the people who were slaughtering had already killed and slaughtered 400 sheep. They had already tied them up in bundles ready to be carried away as soon as we finished. Each person would just come by and carry whichever bundle he was able to carry without wasting any time.

After searching all the houses, we then went to where the planes were parked. We searched them as well but we did not find anything of substance that we liked except the owner's books and those would not have helped us in any way. We were later wishing that some of us were pilots as we could have taken the planes with us to Nyandarua but on a second thought we figured there would have been no landing field up in the mountains, so it would have been all useless. We decided the planes were of no help to us and we decided that the best thing was to set them on fire so that they would not be used to follow us in the mountains and drop bombs on us. The fire that was there as the planes were burning was so big that I do not think that I have ever seen such a big fire ever in my life. I guessed that the fuel that the plane used was stronger than that of an automobile and this may explain why the fire was that big, bright and shiny and reaching far in the heights.

We then picked our bundles of meat and other stuff that we had collected in the houses and started to head back towards our camp in the Nyandarua Mountains. We did not meet any danger on the way and we were safely back to the camp at about half past nine in the morning. When we told those we had left in the camp how things went, they were just shaking their heads with disbelief because they were so confident that we would come back with many guns given the prior surveillance that had been done by our people to locate the place and the guns with the policemen. We told them that we did not think that was our lucky day as far as guns were concerned and that we believed that our God would show us some other place where we would get other guns.

We stayed for quite a long time before we went to invade any other place, but the main reason was because the government had so many of its soldiers all over, especially at the boundary of the forest and the Reserve. There was nowhere that our people would have passed to go and get food in the Reserve given the utmost surveillance by the government troops. We could not even get a way of sending a message to the Reserve to alert our supporters there as to when we could go to collect food.

We encountered continuous hunger because we stayed for over three months before we were able to go to the Reserve or even send anyone because the government army was everywhere and armed to the teeth to kill us on sight. At the end of three months, we finished all our food stock and some people started to run away to the government and others became "Komerera." "Komerera" meant that these people had not surrendered to the government neither were they any longer part of the Freedom army in the forest like ourselves. They used to live in constant fear and in hiding in the place that was called "Kwa Mwanya" (Special Area). They were hiding from both the government soldiers as well as the Mau Mau soldiers. They were really in a lot of danger as they could be targeted by either troop. Any troops (Mau Mau or the government's) that spotted them would kill them instantly. The reason why the Mau Mau killed the Komerera (or, "those lying low") was mainly because occasionally they were captured by the government soldiers and after being punished a lot, they would eventually cooperate with the government soldiers. They were used to bringing the government authorities up to where the Mau Mau lived in the forest given their vast knowledge having been one of us before they became Komerera. With the guidance of the Komerera our people could be attacked unaware of any enemies coming their way and these surprise attacks usually would leave many casualties for our people. It was very bad for our people to lose their lives just like that. That was why we would rather kill one Komerera than risk him bringing the government soldiers who would end up killing many of our people.

After going through many problems as well as constant hunger, General Kago called us where we used to gather for prayers, and after praying, he told us the following: "Given how much the government troops and the administration are surrounding us in the forest, their wishes are we die right here in the forest.

But since we have sacrificed ourselves to die fighting for our country, we cannot agree to die here in the forest. We have to fight with the white soldiers and the white administrators until we are confident that we will get what we are fighting for—our lands and our freedom!"

We were a bit worried especially given that we had gone without food for many days and we felt a bit helpless and weak. On this day when General Kago was talking to us, it was the eleventh day since when we had finished our food supplies. If you looked at any of us, you could not believe that one would last for more than one hour before dying. It was that serious. People had grown weak and emaciated with their eyes sinking inwards. Indeed at that time if the government troops had come to attack us, they would have killed many of us as we did not have much energy to run away. But with God's grace, we did not encounter any attack during this time not even on one day.

After listening to the words of encouragement from General Kago, people regained a bit of their self worth and their spirits were lifted somewhat. Some of the people felt that they would be happy to go to the battle and even if they died while fighting, they might save the lives of others that would have been more helpless. The General told us to stay ready and on the alert as we may be asked to go to attack any time from then. On that day we relaxed all right and had a good day. At about three o'clock in the afternoon, our God did His miracle, which was that there were two cows that had been lost in the forest some time back and nobody knew where they had gone. A man by the name of Mwangi went out to look for bamboo shoots to eat, since this was now what we were eating during this period when there was no food. He came back and brought the news that he had seen the two long lost cows somewhere in an open space right there in the forest near our camp and he made sure he did not scare them because he did not want them to disappear again. These cows were kind of crazy to the extent that if they saw a human being they could just run away just like buffaloes or the deer. They had also had their sanity interfered with by the many bombs that they had encountered. Since they could not hide themselves like the human beings when we noticed planes above us, the cows had been victims of the dropping bombs but fortunately none of them was seriously hurt despite the various wounds that they had received. When Mwangi brought this news, General Kago ordered that those cows should be shot dead immediately. He ordered that they be shot in their heads otherwise if they were shot on other parts of the body they might still be able to run away again and we may never see them again. That is exactly what was done and Mwangi led the other soldiers who were armed and they approached the cows slowly and all at once it was now clear how they could be shot. Waruingi and Muiruri agreed that each of them shoot one of the cows. Immediately they were shot the other people jumped on them and within no time they had been slaughtered and nothing of the cows were thrown away except for the digestive waste ("taatha") and the hooves, and the horns that were obviously not edible. The meat was carried with strong sticks to the camp but if it was not for Waruingi and Muiruri, some people wanted to eat the meat while it was still raw. They were warned that anyone caught eating raw meat would be severely punished.

When the meat got into the camp, the General directed how it would be shared amongst all of us. He asked that nobody should be selfish. Once the meat was cut into pieces, each of us would pick one piece and the leaders were supervising that nobody picked more than one. Nobody wanted to appear like they were being selfish given how everybody in that camp was very hungry. It was also clear that if anyone appeared like the wanted to take more than the others, they would have been injured or killed by the many other hungry people who were all looking for a fair share.

It was very sad if you could see how people were making themselves busy trying either to roast or to boil their piece of meat. You can imagine that the piece each person got was not substantial given that the two cows' meat was to be divided among 1,104 men and women. You actually wonder what a small piece each of us was getting!

As for me, with another young man called Mwangi, we were lucky for we both got the meat on a bone called "karema hiti," meaning "that which defeats the hyena." We were lucky because there were some people who were got only the intestine, or part of the stomach, of the cow or a piece of the liver (all of which were small simple pieces and not satisfying). Those who got those kinds of "meat" did not even take them to where they were sleeping. They just ate them raw on the way. As for me and Mwangi, we were able to combine both our bones after we ate the meat on it and we boiled it to make some soup which was very light and almost like water, but we each drank up to about four cups each. We were able to drink it mainly because we did put some salt to make it tasty. You could not distinguish that soup with ordinary hot water, but there is a Gikuyu saying that says "Mai mahiu matiagaga ugendo," that is, "hot water cannot miss a passage." We boiled our two bones for three consecutive days and added salt to our much diluted soup, but at least it had some taste of meat and kind of filling. Can you imagine the person who got a piece of an intestine with no meat inside, ate it raw and now it was the third day and they had not eaten anything? And this was now the fourteenth day since we had had any food! I am sure you can imagine how such a person was feeling and was looking like.

Chapter 7

Exchanging Our Souls with Food

On the fifteenth day from when we had eaten any real food, it became a very sad day for everybody because our people were really starved and not know what to do. Many felt that even if it meant some people dying, it might be for the better so long as some will eventually get some food; otherwise we might all end up dying of famine there in the forest.

Four hundred of us were selected, among those who were appearing more energetic and stronger than the others, and we were instructed that we had to go to the Reserve and get some food. This was regardless of the many risks that we were already aware existed on the way, yet something had to be done. Our traditional healer prayed for us so that no danger would befall us while on the way to the Reserve and back to the forest. After the prayers, we started our journey headed on the ridge of Mbugiti. We had with us ten rifles and one automatic gun ("gotora"). We went all the way up to the border between the Reserve and the forest, and since it was still in the daylight, we decided that it was better to wait until night fall otherwise if the government troops and the home guards identified us, we might not find our way to the Reserve to look for food. We spied around carefully to find out whether there was anywhere that we could spot our enemies, but we did not see them anywhere. In the evening, at around seven o'clock, we started crossing Kwa Mwanya headed for Mbugiti and at ten o'clock we were at the home of one of our supporters in the Reserve. We immediately told him what was going on in the forest, the hunger and how we had come and he immediately sent out for our other supporters to prepare food for us that we could eat there and what we could carry back to take to our starving people back in the forest. Everything had to be done as fast as possible since we all knew how risky it was for us to be there and we did not want to be identified by the government authorities.

Our supporters did the necessary things very fast and gathered all the food within a short time. By one o'clock that night, all the goods in the form of food that we were to carry back to the forest was already put together. There were fifteen bags of maize, sweet potatoes, bananas and plantains, live goats and four cows. By that time, we had also eaten enough food and we were fully satisfied.

Just that time in the night, we sent five guys to go up to the forest and to bring with them other people who would help us in carrying the goods and also help in slaughtering the goats and the cows near the forest border. We could not go with the animals still alive in the forest as they would betray our movements when their footprints were followed. We had to slaughter them and carry meat with us for our general safety otherwise their footsteps might lead to a surprise attack by our enemies.

We were escorted by some of our supporters and when we got near Kwa Mwanya we asked them to go back, otherwise they might risk meeting with the government soldiers and the home guards on their way up towards the forest for their morning patrol. They might harm them and so it was safer for them to go back while it was still in the night.

We went up to the border of the forest and the Reserve and there we found our "boys" waiting for us. They helped us to carry some of the bundles that we had. The others slaughtered the cows and the goats and they carried the meat. By the time we were there, it was about five o'clock in the morning.

We went on and reached our camp without having faced any danger or en-countering our enemies. The people we had left behind had prepared themselves and were ready to cook the food because they had already got the information that we had found food and it was on the way. When we got there, the cooking started immediately, beginning with the meat, then the maize and beans (githeri) and then roasting of the sweet potatoes and the plantains.

Within a short time, the food was ready and our traditional healer prepared us and led the prayers, thanking God for having guided us safely and for having ensured that we had got food just like we had requested Him in our prayers be-fore we left. People could not believe their eyes when they saw the food that was now ready and we were about to eat it given the many days we had stayed with-out seeing any food at all. It was like a completely new world for us due to the fact that many were about to give and submit to the almost killing hunger that we had gone through. So as to make sure that we had enough food to keep in storage for the immediate future, General Kago ordered that everyone be give food ration of the small cup that was called "wanjika atia," literally meaning "what have you done to me," so-called because of its small size—equivalent to that of a standard water glass or an ordinary cup of tea. Each person was to be given a lot of porridge, which was meant to fill up whatever the difference that the food could not cover. The remaining food was to be put in holes underneath that were dug to ensure safety and a cool storage to give it longevity. Some people were assigned the duty of guarding the saved food as it was feared that some people might eat it while others were not there. Thus, only those with permission could get the food to be shared among all at the same allotted meal times.

The fifteen bags of maize pushed us for between a month or two. After that, the stock started depleting and by that time, the Reserve had grown worse in terms of security as there were more active government troops and their home guards that were out to kill or arrest any identified Mau Mau. The reason why it got worse in the Reserve is because the government authorities and their home guards found out that we had carried some cows and some goats from the Reserve. When they tried to follow them, they did not see them, but they did see the place where we slaughtered them. They tried to follow us in the forest but since we knew how to cover and hide our footsteps, they were not able to follow us up to where we were in our camp, and so they went back with frustrations and tightened the security much more in the Reserve.

General Kago, with our other leaders, decided that it was best for us to go and join the other battalion (group) of our people that was led by Captain Njatha. They feared that the situation might get worse and people might become hungrier if we were not able to go to the Reserve to get food. It was deemed wiser to join the two groups so that in case our enemies attacked us, our numbers might help us in our counter-attack instead of being few and hungry which might expose us unfairly to our enemies who were, of course, very well fed. It was important that we got together to make one strong battalion whereby we could also have had more guns amongst us and more people to handle any battle that might come our way.

One early morning, General Kago called all of to our usual meeting place where he used to address his soldiers and he told us to get ready as we were going to move away from that camp. He warned us to be sure that we did not leave any of our belongings behind since we did not know how long we might stay in the new place that we were going. We prepared ourselves to leave and we started our journey at about three o'clock in the afternoon. On that day when we were moving from that camp, the date was May 5, 1954. We went for quite a long journey and the rain fell quite much while we were still on the way and virtually everyone was very wet. Given that there were no clear paths in the forest, we got more wet from the bushes that we had to walk through especially from the dew that hang on them and through which we had to pass.

We kept going on until it was night and by that time we were along the valley of River Maragua. Since this was a big river and with very high and steep slopes, the people who knew the area asked us to be very careful and to be sure to step carefully where others had stepped. Missing those steps might mean falling quite a distance downwards and if one fell they would be seriously injured or killed by the many rocks at the bottom of this river or by its banks. It was really dangerous and it was made worse by the pitch darkness that had befallen the land at that time. We did keep on going but with a lot of problems including the heavy rains, lots of mud and darkness, not to mention that we were also very hungry. By good luck, all of us were able to cross the river safely without anyone falling to their deaths or any injuries.

When we got on the other side of the river, I found a much steeper hill than the one we had come down on. At that moment, due to hunger and tiredness, I for once regretted why I had come to the forest. I said to myself that had I known that I would come to the forest to face all the problems I had been encountering, especially like the ordeal we were going through of hunger, rain and tiredness, I would not have come. At this time I did not even know how much more we had to go because I did not know where we were going and nobody knew exactly where we were going or where exactly we were at that moment. I was not the only one who regretted coming to the forest on that day as I later learned when many of us talked about the ordeal of that night.

We climbed that hill with a lot of problems and eventually we reached the top looking like wild pigs due to the mud that was all over our bodies from head to toe. Given the steepness of this valley, we were crawling most of the sections holding on to the roots of the trees and the bushes around. This explains why we got so muddy because nobody was seeing due to the darkness that had fully enveloped the land.

We all sat down to rest and by that time it was about two o'clock in the morning. Nobody wanted to hear anything from anybody else and everybody was just feeling like they wanted to sleep right there. General Kago announced that we would not go any farther in that dark and wet night. He instructed us to sleep until the following morning when we would continue to go on looking for Captain Njatha's battalion and that if we did not get them, then we would have to decide on what to do next. Everyone started looking for any reasonable place that they would sleep given the wet circumstances. Some people slept under trees. Others who had tents made from gunny bags, cloth or from cowhides pitched them for the night due to the continuing rainfall. Others had to put up some temporary shelter and they had to cut bamboo in the night so as to make the shelters which had to be close to each other for the sake of security for all. By the time all was done and everyone had some kind of place to sleep, it was already four o'clock in the morning.

We slept at that place and I must say that if anybody did not know that sleep can be really torturous when you have it and you have not slept, I learned that night that one can sleep anywhere when sleep comes. Even though we were so wet, we slept sound and we woke up the following day feeling relaxed from the previous day's long walk.

The following morning, the traditional healer asked us to go and pray to our God as was our daily custom. After finishing our prayers, the healer told us that we would not go beyond that point; we should continue staying there until she speaks to Ngai (God) who would tell her how our situation would be. Nobody could argue with the healer and therefore her instructions were followed to the word. Everyone believed that the healer had the power and privilege to speak to Ngai who guided whatever she said hence we did exactly as she said.

We stayed in that same location for five days, but on the fifth day in the morning, the healer asked General Kago to send thirty of our "boys" to go and look for Captain Njatha's people because she was not seeing them anywhere using her superior visionary ways. She said God was not showing where they were and it looked like they were lost.

The thirty of our soldiers who were selected to go and look for Captain Njatha's people looked for them for three days and wherever they went following footsteps, they would find that they had already left and gone onwards. They followed them until they reached Location 19 and they thought the footsteps were headed for Nyeri. Since they could not keep on going until they found them, firstly, because they did not have enough food, they came back and reported all about their search which really had not identified where Captain Njatha's people were. The traditional healer repeated her earlier words that she could not see them anywhere. The healer said we should leave them alone and she would ask our God what He wanted to do with us.

We stayed in that same location for three weeks still waiting for a word from the healer and there was nothing she said at all. The healer was living in isolation from other people and there was nobody who could go where she was until she came out of there and revealed her communications with the higher spirits.

The period that we stayed there were hard times as far as food was concerned and people started losing confidence with the traditional healer. They felt like the healer wanted everybody to die at that place since she was not showing any new directions that our people would go and not even any ways of getting new food.

One morning at about nine o'clock, a plane passed by on top of where we were staying and circled for a while above us. The plane left after a short while and nobody was really bothered by it since many had been coming and going during our tenure in the forest. After barely half an hour later, we heard loud noises of many planes coming towards where we were staying and nobody had a chance to prepare themselves properly for an escape. Within no time those planes had arrived above where we were and they started dropping bombs on us and the first ones dropped right where the traditional healer was. We saw a piece of the hide skin that the healer was wearing up high in the air and the healer was instantly killed. The healer was just a few yards below us and there was no other way of escaping other than going downwards. The hill was too steep to climb and on the other hand there were not enough bushes or trees to take cover if we went upwards and so we had to go downwards on that very steep valley towards the river bank with all its numerous rocks. People were rolling uncontrollably and if you were unlucky and hit the rocks, you could die or get permanently injured from breaking your legs and ribs. If your head hit the rocks, it would become mashed like a goat's head being prepared for cooking because of the impact of the rocks on the head. Others would be lucky and miss the rocks but could hit the water and sink and by the time you came out you felt like a mad man with total confusion of your whereabouts given that it is something you were not ready for. One would swallow some of the water, or some would flow through ones nostrils and you would come out dazed and confused unable to identify north or south, uphill or downhill. When you got back a little of your senses, you could not stand still after hearing the loud noises of the bombs that were being dropped right near where you were. You could just run up along the river like a mad man especially when you looked at both sides of the river valley and realized that the terrain was very difficult to climb and the risk of being hit by the bombs was much higher if you tried to climb the valleys. There was a constant flow of heavy rocks from the impact of the bombs, which could easily kill someone if you tried to climb up. We were confused and wondered what would save us from this particular ordeal.

What people did was that if they got down to the river safely without having been injured terribly by the rocks, they either went down the river or upwards depending on personal instinct as there was no other choice. Among us were women with children and it is very amazing to report that none of the children was hurt and none died. By the same token, no woman died except for our traditional healer who was a woman named Wandatu. The other forty women were all intact without any severe injuries.

It was very sad to observe right next to you a person falling and being hit so much by the rocks and dying as you watch as you rise from your fall in the waters unhurt. By the time you came from the deep waters with all the confusion, you could not help your friend other than run away for your own soul. It was very frustrating. One would stand up and leave knowing very well that you have left your friend at an almost dying stage but you were equally helpless given the non-stop bombing in the area. Indeed by the time we left that place almost everyone was going crazy because of the loud noises of the many planes and the bombing spree that they were engaged in.

We were spread out in all directions not knowing where the other people were. At that time it was only about nine thirty in the morning, and each person who survived was thinking that they were the only ones who survived because they did not see any one else near them except those who were probably in twos or threes or a few who had ten in their groups. The direction I took was to go upward (northwards) on the river banks, and I had no idea where I would come out eventually but that was not the worry at that time. The issue then was to run away from the bombing as fast as possible and to be as far away from there as my feet would allow. Luckily six other people caught up with me and among those six people, one of them knew the forest pretty well. Indeed he led us from near the top of the Aberdares and took us to the slopes of the mountain where we realized that was now facing Njabi-ini (South Kinagop). We were watching the beautiful scenery down below from up high on the mountain at a place that did not have a thick bush. When I looked at my watch, I realized it was then four o'clock in the late afternoon. We were not talking much as most of were still frightened by what we went through earlier in the day, and we also thought that we were the only survivors out of the many people that were in our battalion.

We were saddened to imagine the death of that many people, and we also did not know where we would go ourselves given our small number.

We stayed there until it became dark, not knowing which direction to go and what to eat or where we would get food. After just being quiet for sometime without anyone saying anything, the man who had led us up to this far, and who was very smart suggested that since we might be the only survivors, we should go to the cultivated forest farms of Kiburu and check whether we might get some potatoes and maize from the farms which we could use as our food.

We did not argue with him and that is what we did and he led us up to the farms. Since it was in the night, we could not know exactly where the potatoes were. What we did was to start in one section and follow up the potato vines and fortunately the owners of those farms had left the potatoes unharvested and it was therefore easy to get enough for ourselves within a short time. Each of us then carried the amount of potatoes their strength would allow them to. Samson led us again back to the forest and we went back safely and when we crossed River Kimakia, he told us we would sleep there. We lit a very good fire and we roasted potatoes which we ate until were very satisfied, and we slept there until dawn. The following morning, Samson suggested that we go up further into the mountain and find out whether we might see any other people from our group who may have been lucky to survive like us. If we saw any, it was well and good and if we did not, then we would know that we were really on our own. If we did not see any of them we thought we might have to go up to Nyeri to try and link up with Captain Njatha's people.

When I heard that we might have to go up to Nyeri, I decided quietly that I would not go to Nyeri myself but I did not disclose this to anybody. I did eventually share my thoughts about going to Nyeri with another man whose name was Kariuki and who had also reached the same decision like me.

We climbed up as per Samson's suggestion but very reluctantly. However, since he was the one who knew the forest pretty well, we could not afford not to follow him lest we would be lost and not find our way out even to go back to our own homes in the Reserve. We went for quite a long distance without seeing anybody or footprints of a person; by the time it was ten o'clock in the morning. Luckily since Samson was very good at recognizing even the slightest indications that somebody had passed somewhere in the forest, he noticed a small kind of human passage through the bushes. He followed that up and we were behind him and after going for another distance, we came face to face with quite a big group of people in which General Kago was one of them as well some of our other leaders like Muiruri, Waruingi and Mbugua and many others who used to lead as well as thirteen women and four children.

We felt a bit relieved and happy to see others from our group whom up to that time we thought were dead. We thought that out of the 1,140 persons, we were the only survivors and that was really saddening. They also thought that they were the only ones who had survived. Their group was 237 people. General Kago told us not to worry about the misfortune that had met us the previous day because when we sacrificed to fight for our country, we knew that those kinds of things were likely to happen; some of us would die, others would be permanently injured and become disabled but in the end, we would get "wiyathi," independence, and our land back that was now owned illegally by the white settlers.

We felt our spirits rising back again after hearing those words of courage from our General, and we all felt once again that we would not stop fighting the white government authorities as well as their home guards until we defeated them. We stayed in that place for two weeks, and thereafter, more of our people trickled in and joined us. At that time, General Kago ordered that all the names of those in our battalion be recorded in the book. Up to that time there was no record and it would be difficult to know who was there and who was not there especially after an unfortunate bombing episode like the one we had just gone through. The recording of the names could give an idea as to how many people may have died from those bombings and if there were others who could join us, then we would have some knowledge of the matter.

By the end of the two weeks that we stayed there we were 840 men and women. After some investigations, it was found that many of our people had died from that bombing massacre. After the two weeks, the leaders decided that it was better that we moved from that location to another one where we might put up a new camp. We carried our belongings headed for Location 1 since we also wanted to find out whether some of our people could have given themselves to the government authorities. If we found out that some had given themselves to the government, then we would know that any time they might bring the government troops who would give us a surprise attack and we would therefore need to be more careful. When we got to Location 1, an area that we were more familiar with the ways of the forest, we built a new camp and by five o'clock in the evening we had finished putting it up. As was our custom, whenever we built a camp, we made sure there were people guarding us from all directions so as to avoid a surprise attack. That was also helpful because we could do our work of building fast and without fear because we knew our guards would alert us of any danger immediately.

After finishing building up our camp, four men came and told us that they had come from the Reserve and that now the security was not as tight as before. They told us they had been living at Kwa Mwanya from the time we were dispersed by those bombs and during the period they were there they did not see any government troops or the home guards searching the area the way they had been doing before we had left for Tuthu.

We were delighted to hear that news and after three days, General Kago arranged how we would go to invade one of the areas in the Reserve, particularly Kiriaini, so that we could get food as our supplies were already depleted. During this time, we did not have a forecaster (healer) among us since Wandatu had been killed, but just before we left for Kiriaini another forecaster (healer) appeared. I have no idea from where she came from; her name was Wanjiru.

When that woman arrived, she called everybody to the assembly and she said that we had to go and invade Kiriaini and that our God would lead us on the way and that we would surely win the battle there without any doubts. She explained that that was why God had sent her to us to tell us about the good prospects we had to win the Kiriaini battle. She said our God had seen and noted how we had dispersed, killed and gone for many days without food.

We did not take any more time and we were arranged in groups and the preparation of how we would go and attack was put in place. We left our Bush, or the Makiama camp, at about three o'clock; we were 400 strong men marching to war at Kiriaini! We got to Kiriaini the following day at about eight o'clock in the night. The reason we took so long is because it is quite a distance from where we were in the forest to go to Kiriaini, and we could also not be able to go and invade that first night and come back the same night. It was far and we would have been extremely tired. Also when coming back, we anticipated having loads of maize, beans, flour and we feared if we met our enemies while that loaded, we might not be able to fight back or to run away. The best strategy was to go and spend the night in Kiriaini in an area that had a thick bush of fern and then we would attack a bit early in the night before it was too late and that way we would still have time to go back towards Nyandarua and be in the forest before dawn.

We were led by one man who came from that area, whose name was Gakui, and he showed us where we would spend the night where we could not be seen by either the government troops or the home guards. At about eight o'clock, General Kago divided us into groups. The first group of 150 people was instructed to go and fight with the home guards; 250 would break into the shops and ransack them of anything valuable that we would need in the forest. They were to carry all sorts of food in the shops. That is exactly how the plan was carried out and within a short period, the battle that was at Kiriaini was so fierce that people did not know what was happening. Within a short time, all the shops had been broken into and the food had been put in gunny bags, maize, beans, peas, cow peas, sugar, cooking oil, salt, matches and everything else that was deemed as of some use in the forest. The only thing we did not want to carry or use in the forest was bath soap. This was important because when we were in the forest we could be able to distinguish somebody who had bathed with soap and our own people in the forest. It was a security measure to avoid the soap. Somebody in the forest who could have bathed using soap would be immediately suspected as having surrendered or part of the government authorities like the home guards who may have infiltrated our battalion.

All the goods we had got from the shops were tied together in manageable bundles for us to carry. By the time we were tying our loot, the sound of guns in the home guards' post was so loud that nobody could really tell what was going on and we could not hear each other due to the loud gun noises. The way the goods had been tied together was such that each person could take at least three large tin-full of maize or beans. This was not too heavy and it was figured that with that weight one could still be able to run away without losing his load even if the home guards were chasing behind him.

We finished our assignments without any problems and all the shops were later set on fire and those who were fighting the home guards in their post did a good job and all of them ran away in the night. As for our troops, we did not lose any except for one man called Ndungu who was shot on the hand but it was not serious. We started our journey heading back to the forest and we had to do that as soon as possible because we knew that the government troops would waylay us. We needed to be out of there fast and at least past Kwa Mwanya where we could engage them in a battle in case they caught up with us up there.

We went for a long distance without hearing any troops behind us or by the path side and since we were not many, we were not able to send some of us ahead to spy for us, as we usually would have done. Inevitably, we found that the home guards and the government troops had gone way ahead of us and they were waiting for us on the way and immediately they started shooting and many of our people were shot dead. We had passed on the ridge of Kiarutara and it is there at Kiarutara that we had been waylaid. When we got near to where the government troops were, they threw grenades at us and started firing and many of us were dispersed in all directions and nobody could help the other except to look for your own personal safety. Since it was a surprise attack and their troops were armed to the teeth with grenades, steno guns, automatic rifles and other sorts of weapons, we did not have time to organize ourselves to fight back and the first instinct was to run away and hide where possible. They were all set and they did not give us a moment to fight back.

In the cause of the forced dispersion, some of our people went backwards from where we had come from, others went to the different sides in search of safety; others went to the banks of River Chania and some fell in the steep sides of the Chania Valley and were injured by the rocks and some died from those injuries. Others became permanently disabled. The group that went backwards, which is the one I was in myself, later on went downwards towards the banks of River Kimakia. We went up along the banks of this river for a long distance and then we eventually went up the ridge and found our way back to the forest without any other dangers. We were arriving at Kwa Mwanya at five o'clock in the morning.

We rested for quite a while and when we felt more relaxed, we started our journey; we got to our camp at ten o'clock in the morning. We sat around waiting for the other members of our troop with the hope that they also found some ways to escape and they would eventually make it to the camp like we had done. Within a short while, some of the others started trickling in small groups. Some did not have their goods and others arrived feeling really sick as a result of the injuries they had received from the rocks when the fell in the steep rocky Chania Valley. As soon as they arrived, our "doctors and nurses" in the camp started to attend to them, while others who had not been seriously injured joined us in the usual chores of the camp.

At the end of three days since the day we had come back, General Kago asked for a roll call so as to determine who did not make it back from Kiriaini because they were shot dead or they fell and were killed by the river rocks or maybe they were arrested. After the roll call was done, it was discovered that thirty men were missing. Immediately after making this discovery, General Kago directed that we would have to move from that camp to another and that we should get ready and carry all our belongings. His concern was that if there were some of our troops who were arrested, they might be forced to come and show our camp to the government troops and that would be disastrous for us. Surprise attacks were the worst and the casualties were usually very high.

Just about then, we picked up our belongings and we were ready to set off. We started our journey at about eleven o'clock in the morning going north towards the mountain tops. At about three o'clock we found a spot that was open there in the forest. We usually knew that such open spots were most likely where the government (enemy) troops might be waiting for us and we usually had to be very careful crossing such an area. We had to investigate it thoroughly and we could only cross when we were sure that there was nobody waylaying us there.

After spying the area carefully and determining that it was safe and free of enemy troops, we crossed it, but just as we were crossing, we heard from a distance behind us sounds of gun shots. General Kago chose 100 strong men who were given twelve guns and they were asked to go back and find out what all that noise was about. The others had to keep on moving ahead to search for the proper site for the new camp.

From that open spot, guards were placed in intervals of about 100 yards from each other until where we were going to build the camp. The reason for keeping the guards in such intervals was to ensure that in case we were still being followed, they would be able to communicate the message fast and our troops would be ready to fight or to hide depending on the circumstances. These guards were also to be responsible to show the 100 men who had gone backwards where the new camp was.

We reached a place that had a small hill and was nicely laid out, and General Kago told us that this was where we would put up the new camp. Since it was getting dark, people started the chores of building the new camp immediately. It was also looking like it might rain any time and it would be very difficult to build the shelters when it was raining.

The kind of construction we made was very simple as it was also deemed temporary. It was therefore not very tiring. We could split a bamboo into two, and then we would remove a cover that was usually at the bamboo joints; and then we would put two bamboos on top of each other; the posts for holding these bamboos were usually three, one at the middle and one each at the ends. We could then put on much lighter bamboo on top. We also had to dig a trench around the shelter to make sure that even if it rained heavily the drainage would go outside the shelter. The shelter was simple and kind of one-sided.

The people who had gone back to find out about the gun shots that we had heard indeed found the government (enemy) troops in the camp that we had just vacated. Fortunately for them, by the time they saw them, they were no longer shooting their guns. They noted some men who had been forced to sit at the bottom of one of the trees around our former camp. After observing closely, they saw three people who had been tied together and immediately they knew that these were the people who had been arrested at Kiarutara and they had brought the enemy troops where they had left us in the old camp. We were very happy and thankful for the wisdom of General Kago who had asked us to leave that camp just a few hours earlier because had we been found there at the old camp, many would have been killed because we probably could not have been ready for the battle that we were not anticipating right at our forest camp.

They had actually tried very much to fool us because at the time they came nobody could have expected them to come inside the forest in the afternoon. Normally they came in the morning and went back in the afternoon. It was very unusual for the government troops to be inside the forest at three o'clock in the afternoon. We guessed that those they had arrested had advised them that the best time to give us a surprise attack be in the late afternoon when they were least expected inside the forest.

Our troops did not bother with them and they were just watching them from a distance and when they finished, they started to head back to go home back to the Reserve. They did not look bothered or suspicious of anything because they probably believed that when they shot guns in the air, anyone who could be around there had run away and so they felt very secure and relaxed.

One of our soldiers told the others that since they did not think the government troops had any idea that they were there, they should each try to shoot one and steal their guns from them since guns were a very essential commodity to our troops as we did not have enough. He also told them that General Kago would be very happy with them if they were able to go back and show some guns that they had taken away from the white soldiers. He also reminded the others of the praise they would get from the people if they brought with them some guns. There were no arguments about those well worded statements from one of our soldiers and immediately they planned for each to shoot one government troop and they identified which each of them would shoot to avoid confusion and wasting the valuable bullets. When the government (enemy) troops finished surveying the area, their leader told them that they could leave for home. Our "boys" set themselves and they agreed that each of them would make sure that they only made one shot at a time. Since it was custom that once they had the gunshot they would take cover so as to get ready to fight back, our boys were not to shoot again. They were to let them fire as many bullets as they wanted to. Our boys were to wait until the enemy troops stood again and they would fire at that time once more and then stop again to find out where the bullets were coming from. Our boys were not to fire then until the enemy troops started walking back home and that would be the time to aim at shooting at them again, aiming at killing each of the targets.

They did exactly that and the enemy troops took cover, all of them lying on the ground and after firing many bullets in the direction that they thought our bullets had come from, they later stopped but realized that no more firing was coming from our side. I guess they thought at that time our troops had run away or they had actually killed all the Mau Mau in the area with the many bullets they had fired. When they stood up to head for home, our troops did as they had agreed upon earlier and fired each at a targeted enemy troop killing them instantly. They then fired again in all directions and after they were tired, I guess they realized that it was getting late and they decided to leave for their home in the Reserve. They knew it would be dangerous for them to be in the forest by night since the veteran Mau Mau who knew the forest very well both during the day and at night would easily overpower them. They also thought we had many guns based on the fact that they did not see us and so they had no idea that we only had twelve guns. Our troops did not quite get to know how the government troops left and they kept waiting for them to fire more shots but they did not and it was then getting dark.

Nobody went near to where those enemy troops were since it had gotten dark and we could not tell whether they were still hiding themselves around there. We also could not tell whether they had laid traps for us using grenades. We decided to go to the camp and come the following morning to check on the situation there and to find out whether we had killed any of the enemy troops. We also had to come with those of our troops who were experts in removing land mines and grenades so as to be sure we were safe.

When we went there the following morning, Mr. Muchiri, Mr. Makumi, Mr. Simon Mwangi and Mr. Samson Kahindi and a few more people conducted a thorough investigation to establish whether they could see a single wire that could have been used to lay traps on us but they did not find any. After the investigation and a thorough search in the area, we found the bodies of the slain government soldiers lying. We thought that is where they would have laid a bomb trap and so we had to do further search but we did not find any. We figured that it could have been difficult for the enemy soldiers to have gotten time to lay the traps given that it was late in the evening and it had gotten dark, so we felt confident that there was no bomb in that area. We found four guns which the dead enemy troops had carried and a few bullets.

General Kago was so pleased for the job well done that previous evening. He was very grateful for the wisdom we had employed. He was particularly happy because he was pleasantly surprised to know that our troops had so much knowledge of the war and especially detonating bombs and disabling the land mines and the grenades. From that day we all learned that we had some very experienced people amongst us who had learned their war tactics during the Second World War (1938-1945) when they had been recruited by the British to fight in Burma in the Indian sub-continent as well as when they were fighting against the Japanese.

During that period, General Kago thought that it was good for those experts to teach our people some of the war techniques that they already had so as to make them more active and to make them proud of the expertise they possessed. General Kago promoted these experts depending on how much knowledge they had. Some became Corporals; others became Sergeants, Sergeant-Majors and also Captains (following the military ranks that were known to exist in the British army).

Those heroes amongst us showed our battalion many war tricks and techniques and especially most of what they had been taught when they were in Burma and other places they had been taken by the British to help them fight against the Germans and their allies. We felt gratified to learn so many war tricks, and we had the confidence then that if the white troops came by, we would be able to fight with them effectively. We kept gaining more confidence by the day given the presence of those heroes among us who were sharing all they knew about the war with us.

Chapter 8

The New Bush

At the time we were in continuous battles with the enemy government troops, we were living at a Bush called Makiama. We lived there for five months and it was while we were there that most of our troops learned how to fire a gun. Before then, none of us knew how to fire a gun and we did not even have the privilege to touch it. We only saw the guns being carried from a distance by those who had them.

We moved away from the Makiama Bush because of the frequent attacks that we got from the government troops and we built a new one that we called Gikumbo, which was on the other side of River Thika. When we got to the new site, as usual we were able to build our temporary shelters pretty fast and within no time, we had finished and everybody had a shelter to live in. There was plenty of bamboo at Gikumbo and that made the construction look like a very easy and simple task. We arrived at the new site at four o'clock in the afternoon. We then started cooking our dinner and by ten o'clock that night, the food was ready and we were served as usual. Almost immediately, everyone fell asleep from the tiredness of the long journey we had taken from Makiama to Gikumbo.

The following morning, as usual, we said our prayers to our God asking Him to ensure that we were out of danger at all times and to give us the strength and the wisdom to fight with the white man until we defeated him and forced him to flee back to his home in Europe. We also prayed to defeat the white man so that we could reclaim our freedom and independence as well regain our occupied lands by the white settler. After staying at Gikumbo Bush for two months, we got short of food supplies and our General instructed that we had to invade one of the home guards' posts so as to grab their guns from them, break into their shops and take away with us all the available food in those stores.

General Kago instructed us to be ready at all times for any day that we may be asked to go and invade the home guards' posts in the Reserve. He also warned us that wherever we would invade next would require very brave and confident men. One day in the evening, we were called to assemble at the place we normally said our prayers. After the prayers, we were told that we would go that evening to invade one of the home guards' posts. We were asked to be ready right then, as we would have to leave immediately.

Our traditional healer said special prayers for those of who were going to invade and after that, 500 of us were chosen and told that we were the ones who would go to that battle. We started our journey headed for the Reserve at ten o'clock in the night.

It took us quite a while before we reached Kwa Mwanya because you could not walk fast in the forest due to the heavy darkness and there was no straight path or road that one could follow. We used to follow paths that had been made by elephants and so it took much longer to reach our destination at two o'clock in the night. We attacked the home guards who were unaware of our plans and were surprised that we could come to attack at that hour of the night.

They thought by then we would be deep asleep inside the forest. Given the way the home guards feared the Mau Mau, they were always on the alert but shivering with fear especially if they heard the dogs in their compound barking. We made the surprise attack on them but apparently this was not their night and their God was still with them, for none of them died as they were able to escape from the post where they left it bare of any human beings. How they did it was a surprise to us but we later learned that there was a rear gate, which our spy had not been able to spot. Since while they were fleeing we were right behind their heels, they were not able to carry most of the things in the post, other than their dear souls. We found three automatic rifles and many bullets and most of their clothing, as it appeared that some of them escaped naked.

We were not angry at our spy for having not identified the escape gate mainly because we knew how risky intelligence work was for our people at that time. If it had been known that he was spying for the Mau Mau, he would have been killed immediately by those home guards.

We had been divided into three groups: one group was to raid the home guards' post, the other one was to break and raid the shops and the third one was to cut trees and lay them on the road so as to make them impassable just in case the enemy troops would try to follow us using their vehicles. It was obvious that sooner or later the colonial army would learn that we had invaded the post and would come following us in their vehicles and so we had to make it difficult for them to catch up with us. The loud noise of our gunshots as we raided the post would invite the attention of the enemy troops. There was no other way for guarding ourselves from the enemy troops but to lay down huge trees on all roads that they might pass while coming to chase us towards the forest. Our assistant had to stay near the locations where the huge trees were on the road so as

to pass information to the rest of our troop informing us that we were being followed. This way we would be ready to fight with them and if we felt like we
were not ready to fight, then we would come up with ways of avoiding them to
avoid any casualties on our side.

Each group worked very hard to accomplish its mission and within a short
time, we were finished with our assignments and were ready to head back. We
also knew exactly where the trees had been laid and we knew the people who
were laying them down were back with us as well as those who had gone to
break into the shops. We did not want to leave anybody behind, as they would
be in danger. Everyone also had to carry his or her bundle of the goodies that we
had just looted headed back to our camp in the forest. Those with guns had to
walk at the back of the pile of our troops so that they could fire in case we were
being followed by the enemy troops. While they were engaging the enemy
troops, those with the food would keep on marching ahead towards the camp,
that way at least the food would reach its desired destination. In front of the pile
of our troops, about four or five men with guns were chosen to lead the way and
their task was to fight any enemy troops who may have waylaid us and they
would fight them until those behind arrived to assist them and the food would be
guarded safely. Such careful security measures were very important.

We started our journey back headed for the forest and on that day we did
not face any danger at all and we went back to the forest where we arrived at
eleven o'clock in the morning very safely. We found the other people we had
left behind to guard our Bush awaiting us with anxiety and expectation of food
from the Reserve. They were very hungry and so any signs of food would be
very relieving. When we arrived back at our camp, General Kago was very
pleased with us and he profoundly praised Captain Muiruri and our other superiors who had led our soldiers who went to invade the home guards on the previous night. The food we brought in that day included 120 bags of maize, thirty
bags of beans and other stuff like salt, matches, cooking oil and paraffin as well
as other little things that would have been necessary in the camp.

After living in Gikumbo Bush for about four months, we were one day invaded by the white enemy soldiers as well as their home guards and from that
day onward, I have never forgotten the events that took place. During all the
time that I had stayed in the forest, I did not possess a gun, and I used to feel that
I had to get my own gun one day. It was, however, very difficult to get a gun
because you had to forcefully get it from an enemy soldier and the opportunities
were always not there. Since I was just a soldier without any rank, just a consta-
ble, those men who had guns used to give us various orders to carry out and you
had no choice but to do what they ordered you to do because you knew they
were the ones protecting you from the enemy with their guns.

I was ordered by one of those men with guns whose name Samuel Mwangi
to stuff an African sausage, called "ngerima," of a cow that had been slaughtered the previous day. I was to stuff it with various kinds of meat as well as
crispy meat from the cow fat and I was to make sure that it was fried in oil and

dried completely as part of preservation because it would have to be eaten for a number of days.

I did exactly as I had been ordered to do and after cooking that "ngerima," I took it to where Mr. Mwangi was lying down resting. He asked me to cut a piece from the thinner side which I did and I left him lying down there and I went down below to the river so as to wash my hands. I put my piece of the "ngerima" in my kitbag without even having a bite. When I started washing my hands, I saw as if a lightning had just passed and I thought I was dreaming or in a daze. I cannot even explain clearly what was happening but I heard loud noises like the kind made by thunderstorms and I could not identify the source of these loud noises. When I looked behind where I had come from, I could not believe my eyes for I saw Mr. Mwangi up high in the air as if something had thrown him up and then he just fell down like a log. When he fell down I saw right at his feet a white man and next to him two men who were dressed in the kind of clothes Mau Mau used to wear.

I was not able to observe clearly because when I saw a white man, just a few yards from where I was, I knew that I was facing an enemy. It was only my God who would help me because if he saw me, there was no alternative but to be shot dead. It was like the blink of the eye, but I had to duck into the river and I went upstream quiet and fast and much later I came out of the river and went to the side with the rest of our troop members. I did not know where I was and I was alone. I could also hear gun shots and bombs but they were quite a distance from where I was at that time.

I went up in the direction that I thought I might see some of our people and luckily through God's will, I met quite a sizable group that had also fled the scene at Gikumbo and they were also lost just like me. These people were the ones who were now telling me that there might be very few survivors because we had been surrounded from all sides and the enemy troops were very many. They had been brought there by the Surrenders, and one of them was a fellow called Wamikori who had surrendered himself to the government troops because he could not survive the hunger that most of us were going through in the forest.

Our people were dispersed in all sorts of directions. Others were killed and others were maimed and became permanently disabled. That day was filled with sadness and quiet prayers and we lived with constant fear for ourselves and for our comrades whom we feared we had lost to the enemy. We were also hungry and tired and we could not sit still since the planes were dropping bombs from the air indiscriminately and the government troops were chasing us on the ground. It was a very rough day to say the least.

In the evening, people got together so as to find out how many people were missing after taking the roll call, either through death or being captured by the enemy. After the roll call, it was established that more than 200 people were no longer in our group. Since by that time it was night, there was nothing much we could have done but we had to wait until the following morning to do a search for our friends.

The people who had the knowledge of dismantling bombs and grenades as well as entrapping the land mines were sent to go and do that in the area near our former Bush. Samson Kahindi was the lead person in this endeavor as he had a lot of knowledge of how to detonate a bomb. He detonated many and indeed we later on used some of those bombs in the war right there in the forest.

We moved away from that Bush and we went quite some distance away from there. We put up a simple camp and after three days, the traditional healer (seer) asked us to move from there and go to the Gathuki-ini Ridge, otherwise, our enemies would come and invade us again as they were still chasing us. Also, given that we did not have enough food supplies, it would have been dangerous to have the enemy troops and their home guards invading us and snatching all the remaining supplies that we had and there was no telling where we would get the next supply in the near future.

It was about three o'clock in the afternoon by the time our seer was informing us that we had to move. Indeed everybody was asked to get ready with all their belongings which usually included the bags one slept on, or which sometimes were pitched as tents, cooking pots and utensils and any other paraphernalia that one might posses. We went where we had kept our food and we still had forty bags of maize remaining and two bags of beans. It was all shared amongst us so each was carrying a small load of the maize and beans. We then went back to where we were sleeping and we were told to be prepared for an early journey towards Gathuki-ini.

The journey towards Gathuki-ini was very tough, as we had to pass through large bushes where there were no previous paths and yet it had just rained heavily the previous night. So the bushes were very wet and we were all looking like wild pigs because of the way we kept falling in the mud since it was also very slippery due to the wetness. We were also going throughout steep places, as we had to cross a number of rivers on the way, like River Thika, Gita-biki, Ndiara, Githika and many other small ones that were there in the forest.

We started that journey at eight o'clock in the morning and we were led by one of our soldiers who knew that area very well. We did not encounter any problem on the way except for being tired with the journey itself. This was mainly because it took us a long time to move onwards as we had to cover our footprints very well so that nobody could possibly follow us to our final destination. Given that we were many, wherever we passed became like a path that had been used for many months. It was a difficult task to cover our footsteps but we had to do it, otherwise we would be followed by our enemies. In order to cover our footsteps, we would go back the way we had come for one mile and then we would take another route to get to the farthest point we had gone before we went backwards. We would then take a different path going backwards to the last point where we were. After that we would all be asked to take each their own route back to where we had started. We would have liked four different routes from that point which was the idea to confuse anyone who would be following us as they might have to take the four different routes and all of them would take them in circles and bring them back to the same point that they started. The idea was to confuse completely whomever might follow us so as not to know the real direction that we were headed.

After doing all that, we would then walk across the different routes making them look like a cross and by that time we would be walking forwards and by that time, we would be gone ahead for a distance of about six or eight miles just circling one place. After all that, we would then face the direction we were headed and we would erect a tree stump or some bags which we would dress up like a person and we made sure it faced the direction we had just come from (the opposite of where we were going). We would leave it there and when those enemies that might follow us came there and saw this image dressed like a person, the first thing they would do was to fire profusely thinking that they were firing at the Mau Mau. After they fired and found no movement, they would then approach our fake image and realizing it was just a made-up stooge, they would go back in the direction it was facing, which is the opposite direction of where we were heading. After following the many routes we had already created, they would find themselves coming back to the same location that they started.

While they were still doing their rounds there not knowing which way to follow, they would get frustrated and tired, and then sometimes it would be almost nightfall and they had to go back home. The many routes we created confused them and they usually would give. By that time, we would have gone very far to our desired destination making similar confusing routes as we went along.

We kept going for the whole day but we still did not get to Gathuki-ini as we got too tired and hungry at the same time. When we reached at River Githika, we decided that we would spend the night there. We started building a small temporary camp and we started cooking, as everybody was very hungry.

At ten o'clock that night we assembled together to say our prayers as usual and after the prayers, we were served food and we started to eat. We were not very happy with ourselves given how tired we were, but each of us had to remember why we had sacrificed our lives in the forest and so we had to keep on persevering. Our food rations were very small as we almost always never had enough food supplies and since there were so many government troops in the forest and in the Reserve, we had to do with the little that was available. The worst years in the forest, when the government troops were consistently on our heels and made it difficult for us to go to the Reserve to get food, were 1954-1956.

Given the way our people were tired, we stayed at that location for two days so as to allow people to be more rested. We were also waiting at that location for some of our people that had been sent to the Reserve to spy on how the situation was there. If the situation had improved, they could identify where food would be gotten and some of our soldiers could be sent there to bring it in the forest. On the evening of the second day, some of our soldiers that had been sent to the Reserve arrived at our temporary camp. They brought bad news to us for they told us that the thirty soldiers that had been sent to go and spy in the Reserve found that they had been waylaid by the government troops and their home guards and they made a surprise attack on our soldiers, unfortunately killing five of them. The others managed to escape and they brought us the news. They also told us that the Reserve was being very closely watched by the enemy soldiers and their home guards and that it was not easy at all to try and penetrate the Reserve as most people would be killed at the Kwa Mwanya. The enemy soldiers had covered almost every possible route that we could possibly make from the forest to the Reserve, and they had even laid traps on the way as well grenades which would be lethal to us. Most of them were stationed at the forest edge at the boundary between the forest and the reserve in the Kwa Mwanya.

When our heroes told us about their encounter, General Kago felt very sad because he could tell that our food supplies continued to dwindle. He feared the consequences on his troops because they might get too hungry and start despairing and questioning whey they ever came to the forest. Some might even consider surrendering to the colonial administration so as to save their own individual souls. Immediately after hearing the bad news, General Kago called a meeting in our usual prayer location. Mr. Philip Kimunyu led the prayers. The prayers he led were both of sadness as well as confidence building, and they went as follows:

Ngai wa Gikuyu na Mumbi thai

[God of Gikuyu and Mumbi—Praise God]

Tuteithure mokoini ma Thu thai

[Release us from the enemy's hands—Praise God]

Tuhe hinya Na ugi hari Thu ciitu-thai

[Give us strength and wisdom over our enemies]

Tungihotwo Ni Thu, ti ithui twahotwo, Ngai witu niwe wahotwo

[If we are defeated by the enemy our God, it is not us who are defeated but you yourself Lord]

Tungihotana ti ithui twahotana niwe wahotana ngai witu-thai

[If we win, it is not us who have won but it is you our God who has won. Praise God]

Thai, thathaiya Ngai Thai (x 3)

[May the Lord be praised (x 3)]

After the prayers, General Kago told us to get ready for we would have to continue with our journey to Gathuki-ini the following day. He feared that we might stay there much too long and our enemies might invade us; given how weak the people were because of hunger, our soldiers might not be in a position to fight the enemy.

We had a sad night partly because we were hungry and also due to the sinking spirits that we had then after hearing the news about our five killed brothers and also being told how bad it was with the many government troops being everywhere. We did not know where our next food would come from. Indeed we later learned that some of our soldiers who liked their stomachs very much escaped from our camp that night and went to surrender to the enemies (the colonial administration).

The following morning, we prayed to our God as was custom and our traditional seer led us with her visionary guidance assisted by other people who had some knowledge of where we were going. That journey was tiring and as usual we had to keep going in circles so as to hide our footsteps; it took long before we reached our destination partly also due to the thick bushes that we had to go through. People started despairing and almost getting annoyed with the circumstances we were going through.

After covering all our movements, we headed for Gathuki-ini where people did not know where it was except for a few of us who were familiar with the area. Most of us were just following like goats without knowing where we were going and what to expect once we got there. We again went for another whole day until it got dark before we reached where we were supposed to have been going. It got dark just after we had crossed River Irati. When we got there, our foreseer said we should not move beyond there and that we should build our camp there until she was advised by our God where He wanted us to go from there. Since most people were tired and hungry having gotten there around eight o'clock at night, we did not build our camp that night. We had no idea where to get the bamboo at that hour of the night and it was extremely dark. The forest in the night looked like a dark cave.

We slept at that location with a lot of problems—being wet as it was raining hard, being tired, being hungry; even though we still cooked that night and ate, nobody was really happy at all with the situation we were in.

Chapter 9

Gathuki-ini Bush

When I say that you do not need to be old to have seen a lot of stuff in this world, or to use the Gikuyu saying, "Kuona uriru ti gukura," I know exactly what I am talking about for by the time we were experiencing all what I have been describing above, I was only twenty-two years old.

The following day we started by building our camp at this Bush that we called Irati and this location was rather unique as it was between two rivers enclosing it like an island. The two rivers met there and if one went upwards, you would hit the river and likewise if one went downwards. So our camp was in a location that was shaped like a V and we were in between.

We built up the camp until we were done and people chose who to live next to based on their social networks, that is, how long they knew each other and whether they were friends or whether they were from the same place of origin in the Reserve. But I must emphasize that what was most important is the unity of everyone in the camp so that we could help each other effectively and efficiently in case we were attacked by the enemy.

We stayed at Irati Bush for a period of five months without being given directions to move out of there by our traditional seer. We started having our spirits back up high since the Reserve was getting a bit freer and the high security grip that existed five months ago was being relaxed a bit which meant we could be able to go and look for food in the Reserve. We were able to find that our assistants in the Reserve had gathered food, goats and cows for us to bring into the forest as our food. We also got supplies of medicine and clothes, which we desperately needed. During the period that we stayed at that Bush, we were aware that the people who had escaped from our group had surrendered themselves to the colonial troops and they may bring them any day any time for a surprise attack on us. We had to keep our guards on duty on all the routes that could possibly lead to the camp to be sure to report any forthcoming enemies. Only five guns were usually left to guard the camp, and the guards who were manning the possible routes to the camp that the enemy might use had all the others.

On the fifth month during the period that we stayed at Irati Bush, two amazing things occurs which I will never forget and possibly nobody who was in that camp will ever forget. The first thing was that, one morning, eight of us went to guard the routes leading to the camp and we had three guns with us. I did not have a gun myself, but I did have a sharp sword and a machete. Another man named Joel had a sword and a sharp spear. At the place that we all sat, there was a huge oak tree that had fallen there and it looked like a thick fence between the other side and us. No bullets fired from the other side could penetrate this huge fallen oak tree and so we felt protected from the other side in case of an enemy attack thanks to the fallen tree!

While we were just sitting there talking in low voices as we could not talk loudly just in case there were enemies nearby, I turned my head and all at once I could not believe my eyes for I saw a white man not very far from where I was coming towards us. It was not clear at that time whether the white man and his troops had seen us. We could not understand why we had not seen them earlier. I turned to my colleague, a man named Mwangi wa Kabarai, and I told him, "Mwangi, there is a white man!" When Mwangi turned and saw the white man, he could not believe it and he immediately decided to fire at him, otherwise, he feared if he came too close to us, they would arrest us and we would be in deep trouble with possibilities of being shot dead or sentenced to hanging. Mwangi spared no time and within the time of an eye's blink, Mwangi had fired at the white man. The bullet hit him in the neck and he went up and fell down like a huge gourd full of water falling from the air.

At that moment, the white troops took cover by lying on the ground and firing many shots and the noise in the area from the gunfire was too loud to comprehend anything anybody was saying. It was just the loud noises and the smell of burning ashes from the gunfire. The colonial troops fired very many shots but since they were not sure where the bullet that killed their fellow white man had come from, they were just firing aimlessly in all directions. After continuously firing bullets for about forty minutes, they paused for some minutes. During that period, Mwangi, Kageche and Kangara fired three other bullets towards the white soldiers and they started another round of continuous firing. At that time, I did not know exactly what happened but one of the bullets came through Mwangi's gun through the lock and it hit him on the shoulder. Fortunately it was not fatal and in fact it did not penetrate to his bones but it was only on the muscle surface.

When Mwangi told us that he had been shot, another man we were with whose name was Chege took Mwangi's gun but after trying to put back the bullets, it was not working well as it had already been messed up at the lock. The colonial troops continued to fire aimlessly in all directions. We could not leave where we were hiding as we had a very good protection from the fallen oak tree and if we left that hiding place, there was no doubt that we would have been shot dead at once.

Since the white soldiers thought that it must have been a big battle, their bullet count started going down given the many that they had fired, and they thought it wise for them to flee the area. They had to carry their dead soldier and run away as they had no clue how many Mau Mau were engaging them in the "battle." They did exactly that and they picked the dead body and started running away. Kangara and Chege both agreed to fire and kill at least one soldier each. Just then, Kangara shot dead one of the soldiers who had been carrying the dead body, but Chege was not successful and he did not shoot any of the white soldiers.

When they saw that another one of them had been shot dead, they dropped the dead body and took to their heels running away as fast as they could from the scene. We were watching them as they ran away and disappeared towards Kwa Mwanya and we did not see them again. We approached the dead white soldier who had been dropped by his friends. We removed his clothes and we learned that he had a bullet-proof vest; we realized that had he not been shot in the neck, he would not have died. We did not have time to remove his bullet-proof vest because just about that time, airplanes started hovering up in the air near to where we were and it was our time to take cover. We had to run away from there because we knew very well that when the planes start dropping bombs, that area would be swept clean killing everything around there.

We went up very fast towards the camp. When we got there, we found General Kago waiting for us to brief him of what we had seen and we told him of our encounter. Immediately he ordered 200 of our soldiers to go to the location that we had been. They were equipped with ten guns and other weapons.

Mr. Mwangi had not been shot badly except his flesh was burned, but our doctors there in the forest were very good at attending such bullet wounds. He was treated at once and he really never got sick and after a few days he was fine; he joined the others in the daily chores of the camp and the forest. The soldiers that General Kago sent could not go back to the same location that we were at because the many bombs that had been dropped had swept that place clean. They were observing that location from a distance. Fortunately no white soldiers or their home guards came back to the forest on that day.

We continued to guard the routes to the camp every day and night and we did not get into any trouble. We started feeling complacent and thinking that no enemy troops would come to invade us in this camp especially after experiencing one of their own being killed by the Mau Mau despite having been fully clad in a bullet-proof vest. I guess they were concerned and worried as to what kind of gun this was that could kill somebody even while that heavily protected. The second thing was that just before the five months expired while we were still at the Irati Bush, people were just sitting idly chatting away; others simply basking from the sun; others killing lice from their clothes and their bodies, especially the hair; others smoking tobacco; others at the place we used to pray wanting to talk to the traditional seer; and others just walking up and down, here and there in the camp.

Myself and a few others like Joel, Kagera, Gidraf, Mwangi Makara and many others that I may not need to write their names down, were resting on side of the Irati River and that was like the edge of the sharp slope of the river. It was difficult to get there because even when we initially came there we had to go down quite some distance before we found our way back there given how steep it was. We were just talking and then we saw one airplane coming from the northern side passing swiftly towards the south. It disappeared for a few minutes and then it came back and went northwards and that time it took about ten minutes before it came back again. By that time we knew how to hide ourselves from being seen from above by those searching us from the planes. We knew that the planes could identify us from the ground through contact with our eyes, and also any kind of fire smoke; we also knew that fingernails and toenails were also easily identifiable, as well as anything metallic like a machete (panga), a sword, a spear as well as a gun. These are the things we had to hide fast in case we noticed a plan hovering over us.

After the ten minutes, the planes that were above us were many and uncountable. From where we were sitting, we could not get any time to go downwards the way we had come to that spot and where the slope was not as steep. We could also not get time to go back to where we used to sleep to get our belongings although we always carried our essential wherever we were, as we knew there was always the danger of being invaded at any time. If one did not carry their essentials, they risked leaving behind their clothes and their bedding and this would expose one to a lot of cold. One also risked leaving their food behind and this would have been bad, as you would never tell where the next food would be found. So at least we were not completely bare.

The airplanes started to drop bombs. Others were firing bullets at us from the air, as there were a number of jet fighters that were hovering above us. The loud noise that was there was immeasurable and only someone like me that was there to witness can possibly explain. It was deafening to the extreme!

People were dispersed in all sorts of directions, others were killed, and others were buried alive by falling rocks from the bombing that was going on and to others that died from bullets from the jet fighters. The bad thing and also a shocking one was that everybody had to go through the steepest side of the river. It was the only one that was seemingly safe and there was no time to try and go the way people had come there originally given the confusion in the air and everywhere with the bombs falling like rain. Everyone was just trying to save himself or herself and there was no time to check on the welfare of others. It was "every one for themselves and God for all of us!"

We were rolling over the steep slope face downwards but by the time you got to the middle, a huge root of one of the trees around could turn your head around and it would be facing upwards by the time you reached the bottom. You could then be turned around and you would go rolling like a log and you could then fall into the river just like a rock or a tree trunk. The section of the river my friends and I fell into was very deep and if one did not know how to swim, they would have just drowned or washed away to a waterfall that was just a few meters ahead of where we fell. Any one who was washed by the water to that fall had their bones broken by the rocks on the waterfall and they died. Others became permanently disabled.

As for us, we could hit the deep end of the section of the river that we fell into and then come up. We could try to find assistance to ensure that we got out of the river. When we got out, I looked back and I could not believe the steep hill behind that we had just come through. I could not examine it well as the sound of the falling bombs was both deafening and scaring, hence running away from there was the most logical thing to do and not to be mesmerized of the steep hill behind us. Each and every one was going on their own way once they came out of the river as there was no time at all to find out what happened to the other people around you. The bombs falling and the rocks, which made loud noises, like that of thunderstorms as well as the bullets from the jet fighters that were falling like rain pouring on earth as if with a vengeance.

When we came out of the river with another man called Gicharu, and a number of other people, we went northwards (or upwards) following the river bend. We went up for quite some distance without knowing where we were going or where we were. It was about three o'clock in the afternoon that we finally took some rest. Since we were way up high on the Nyandarua Mountains, we had a beautiful view of all sides of the Gikuyu land (Central Province). We could also see clearly the sides of North and South Kinagop. The only side we could not see very clearly was the side of Nyeri.

We were fourteen of us who took a rest at that place trying to decide where to go after the rest. We did not know how we would end up hooking up with the other people who may have survived like us. After resting for about two hours up to five o'clock in the evening, Gicharu suggested that we go downwards to the side of Njabi-ini, and if possible, he suggested, we should go all the way to North Kinagop. He told us that if we got to North Kinagop, he would show us the ways there which could lead us to places we could get food. Fortunately among us was Mr. Kang'ara and he had a gun. We felt protected at least with one gun in our midst.

We kept going downwards until we reached Njabi-ini where we found herders of both cattle and sheep, which were owned by a white settler whose Gikuyu nickname was Mr. Ciithi. I could not tell his actual name, but I suspect it must have been Mr. Sheath and the Gikuyu had corrupted it to Ciithi, which was more convenient to pronounce in Gikuyu. Such nicknames were commonly given to the white settlers by their Gikuyu laborers to describe how their bosses looked. For example, if he was tall, he might be nicknamed "mrefu" which was

Swahili for tall, if he had beards, he might be nicknamed, "materu," Gikuyu for lots of beards; sometimes their difficulty in pronouncing English names might be corrupted and localized to fit a Gikuyu pronunciation like "sheath" for "Ciithi."

We got at Ciithi's at about seven o'clock in the evening, and they were just enclosing the sheep in their bomas where they slept in the night. At that moment, Gicharu told us that we had found some food to eat and that we should wait for the herders to lock up the sheep and leave and we would go in and carry as many sheep as we would be able to. We did just like Gicharu had suggested, hiding somewhere we could not be seen. We hid behind a very thick poison ivy, so thick that nobody could think any one could go in there. At nine o'clock that night, Gicharu asked us to get out of our hiding place and once we got into the sheep pen, every one should take as many sheep as they could, be it four, two or just one depending on your energy.

When we got to the sheep, I was able to carry only two sheep. You had to slash their stomachs open and get rid of all the intestinal and other stomach organs inside the sheep and be sure to carry only the external parts of the sheep, which could provide for more meat. You also had to cut off the head and then just carry it without slaughtering it until you reached wherever our destination in the forest would be. The sheep were heavy as they were the high breed kind that produces wool, and these tended to be heavier than the traditional breeds. The others carried three except for Joel alone who was able to carry four of them. He was, however, able to carry those many because he had a bag and he put them in the bag and that made it easier to carry.

Everybody struggled to carry their load of sheep until we got some place where Gicharu told us we might be able to get some ropes from the forest to tie the sheep and make them less cumbersome to carry. I had tied up mine with the blanket that I covered myself with while sleeping because there was no way I could leave the sheep knowing how hungry we had been for so many days and here was meat! I would rather have tied them up with my pants and I go half-naked but be sure the meat was headed for the forest.

We got some strong ropes from some trees there in the forest and we all tied up our load quite well making it more comfortable to carry and thereafter Gicharu led us back to the forest. At one o'clock in the night, we got to a place that had less vegetation; Gicharu identified the place and he told us that we would not get lost again as he now could remember that area. He told us that he and his friends were sawing timber in that area before the war in 1948.

Since Gicharu knew the geography of that area very well, we were very happy, as we knew we could not get lost again. He even told us that if we wanted to go to our homes in the Reserve, he would guide us up to there. He was so confident with his old environment. He asked us to make fire and roast our meat without any worries. Some of us had to look for firewood while the others slaughtered the sheep.

Within no time, the fire was ready and the meat had been put on the fire and since we were hungry, the meat was being roasted with open fire so as to cook fast. We did not even mind the smoke and indeed some were even eating the meat raw. After one hour, everybody was full from the meat and what we then wanted was some water to drink as were thirsty. Gicharu showed us where we could fetch water and within a short time we were all full and we had quenched our thirst and the only thing we wanted now was to sleep.

Mr. Gicharu advised us that we would not sleep there, as there was a big chance that the owner of the sheep might find us. He feared that given the way we were tired and the night being late too, there was a chance that we might oversleep in the morning and the owner might find us right there sleeping and we would be in deep trouble as we would either be arrested or killed and that would be very bad and a loss we did not want to encounter.

As I mentioned above, we knew the art of hiding the footsteps there in the forest and we started doing that from that point where we had roasted our meat. Since we were not very many (only fourteen of us), we were able to cover our footsteps in such a way that anyone following us would just keep going around and coming back to the same spot.

We kept going on until we crossed River Kimakia and then we went up-wards and then northwards for quite a long distance. We covered our footsteps and then got to a place that had little vegetation and went a bit to the north of it. At that point we decided we would spend the night there. We agreed that seven of us would guard the others who would sleep until midday and then the other seven would exchange and would guard those who were to sleep until evening or whenever they would no longer be sleepy. I was one of those who would do the guard duty in the morning. At about ten o'clock that morning, some of those who had slept in the morning started to wake up and we exchanged with them and they guarded us so that we could also sleep. By three o' clock that dat, all of us had woken up and we felt we had had enough sleep. We started asking each other what we would do after that, where we would go, how we might get to see the other people from our group and what we might do if we missed them. In the end, Kang'ara, Gicharu, Kagera and Muchiri suggested that if we did not get the other people, we should go up to Nyeri where our General Commander-in-Chief, Mr. Dedan Kimathi was stationed. We would pass along North Kinagop and keep on going until we came to Nyeri. There was no argument raised to this suggestion because we all knew very well that if we thought of making rounds at Kwa Mwanya we would be risking a lot and we might be shot dead by the ene-mies especially because we only had one gun with us and it had only five bullets remaining. That would not have protected us in case we came face to face with the government soldiers. We probably would have only fired once or twice while on our way running for escape.

At the time we were discussing these issues, it was at five o'clock in the af-ternoon. We decided unanimously to stay at the same place for a week with the hope that we might be joined by some of our people. We would continue feed-ing on our meat and we also agreed that if we did not find anybody else, we would go back to Mr. Ciithi's and steal more sheep, which would become our food, while on our journey towards Nyeri. We stayed at the same place for two more days. It was a secure place as we would be able to see anyone coming from all directions. We were sure that anyone passing there be they the Mau Mau or the government troops would have to pass across that open field, and we knew we could not miss them.

On the second day at about six o'clock in the evening, while at our guard duty station near the place we were sleeping, we saw some Mau Mau people, numbering about 200, closing that open veldt going towards Njabi-ini. Gicharu gave them the special Mau Mau signal, which was hitting the sword against a stick and when it makes a sound, then the Mau Mau would know those are fellow Mau Maus. That is what Gicharu did and they responded positively and then he made another signal inviting them to come along and they came up to where we were.

There was a lot of happiness that we all witnessed after meeting our people again. The new ones who had joined us were particularly overjoyed when they found that we had meat given how hungry they were. Indeed, we sympathized with them a lot and given our common philosophy while in the forest that if a bean fell, we would share it among us, we were ready to give them all the meat we had and they all shared it well and at least everyone had a piece. They could not get satisfied given that they were many and we had not left so much since it had been our food during the previous days.

We talked and shared many different stories and things we had seen since we unceremoniously parted at Irati Bush where we were dispersed by the bombing planes. Some were telling us that General Kago was shot on that day but there was nobody who could verify the facts. Just about that time after eating, it was decided that some of our soldiers should go to Mr. Ciithi's and get more sheep and if possible bring the cows as well so that we could have some food that could last us for a little longer time. One hundred and fifty men were selected to go to Ciithi's and raid so as to bring as many sheep as was possible. They were to be led by Gicharu who knew the way quite well.

When they got at Ciithi's, they found that the whole place had been surrounded by electric wire, but since we had clever people who knew many things, they did not have any problems and they simply cut those electric wires and they were ready to take the sheep. They removed 200 sheep and led them towards the forest. Before they got to Kiburu River, they agreed that they should slaughter all the sheep and carry them as meat instead of alive as they were then. They feared they might be followed and with all those sheep, it would not be very difficult to identify the way they had followed. They slaughtered all the sheep and they carried the meat.

They got back to the camp where we were at about three o'clock in the morning and immediately we started cooking all the meat; within two hours, all the meat had been cooked and everyone had eaten to their capacity. The following morning, we agreed to leave that location, just in case we might still be followed and we knew very well that they had to follow those many sheep. We did not want to chance a surprise attack; on the other hand we did not have enough guns that we could have used to fight back with the army and the police who would have come to follow the sheep. At that time, we only had five guns, three rifles and two automatic guns and a few bullets. We left that location at about nine o'clock that morning being led by Gicharu and Muchiri since they were the ones who knew that area well.

We kept on going southwards until we reached a place, which I led them, calling it Kinyagana. We arrived there at about five o'clock that evening, and we were told to put up a camp right there and wait for a few days to see whether we might be able to find some of the other people in our battalion who were still missing. We knew that not all of them were dead and we figured they would have to come back to this area since it is the one they knew best.

After three days, General Kago came with a huge group of people, numbering 540. When they found us, we could tell they were very hungry and we gave them all the meat that we still had remaining for them to eat. While we were still in that location, General Kago sent our spies in all directions, some towards the Reserve and others towards Njabi-ini, to find out which area would be our next target to look for food. We had to do that even if it meant engaging the government troops in a battle lest people would die of hunger in the forest.

The spies did a good job and brought back their reports on time. Those who had gone towards Njabi-ini came and told us that the sheep and cattle for Mr. Ciithi were being guarded by some Maasai warriors and some policemen and they were housed in a small post right near the livestock.

Those who had gone towards the Reserve brought the news that Kwa Mwanya was at that time free of any government troops or any home guards. It was clear and we could ably pass through to go to the Reserve. They told us the government troops and the home guards were stationed at the home guards' post. When General Kago had this news, he immediately decided that our troops had to go and get some food.

General Kago selected 400 people who would go to get food. They were also divided into two equal groups, one to go to Njabi-ini and the other one to the Reserve. The one that was to go to Njabi-ini was instructed to go and attack Mr. Ciithi's farm and fight with the Maasai and the police and come back with cattle and sheep as many as they would be able to bring. I was in the group that was to go to Mr. Ciithi's. The other group was to go to the Reserve to bring back maize and beans and whatever else they were able to find that they knew we would need in the forest.

When we started to go to Mr. Ciithi's, we arrived there at about nine o'clock in the night. Captain Waruingi led us and we had seven guns with us. When we got there, we went in through the main gate of the post instead of going through the back door. When the policemen saw us, they started firing their guns and we started shouting at the top of our voices just as we had planned. Since we were many, the loud voices were drowning them and this was the idea to scare them to think we were too many for them to handle. During our shouting, we were making scaring phrases like "cut him up," or "I have the head," "I have the leg," "I have the gun," and many other scaring cries to fully intimidate the policemen and the Maasai warriors and to confuse them totally. They could not even know which way to run away because we were shouting from all sides of the post. In a short while, we heard those firing guns from quite a distance away from the post. At that time we knew that we were not in luck because sooner or later there would be government troops coming there to help the policemen who would be called by telephone from Naivasha. If we did not hurry and leave the area immediately, we might be found right there by the enemy troops and everything would turn out to be a disaster. Captain Waruingi directed that we carry the sheep as soon as possible and leave the area as fast as our legs would carry us. When he gave those orders, our people started cutting the stomachs of the sheep open and poring out all the inner stuff so as to make the sheep lighter to carry and within no time everyone had their load ready to go. We carried other things from there like clothes, bullets and shoes as well as cooking pots and any canned food that the police had kept for themselves there in the post.

We started going back towards Nyandarua facing no problem and eventually we got back safely to our camp. We got back there at about four o'clock in the night. General Kago ordered that all the meat be cooked so that our hungry troops could be fed and also so that the people coming back from the Reserve would find ready meat. After a while those who had gone to the Reserve also arrived with twenty bags of maize and forty cows! We were overjoyed because we now knew that hunger was no longer with us and all that was remaining was to concentrate on fighting the white man and his troops as well as the home guards. General Kago kept spies on all sides of our camp to ensure that no enemy would come to our camp unannounced. We were also ready to fight with them any time they would invade us.

Those two Bushes, Irati and Gathuki-ini, saw many of our troops die because of the surprise attack that we encountered there. It was very demoralizing but we had to keep remembering why we were in the forest and so we had to keep on persevering and fighting on with the hope of winning and chasing the white man out of Kenya. We needed our land and freedom back!

We stayed there for a month and after one month we moved to another Bush that was called Kanyekiini where we stayed for three months. We got disturbed at times while we were at this Bush by planes that could drop bombs on our people. They would get hurt but not so seriously. We had our "doctors" there amongst us who took care of those kinds of injuries and those injured were treated and they healed quite well.

One morning at about nine o'clock, government troops were brought by some Surrenders but since we had our spies on all sides, they were spotted from some distance and the news was relayed to the camp immediately. General Kago arranged 300 of our soldiers with seventeen guns to be ready and he ordered that those government troops had to be engaged in battle. That is exactly what was done and within a short while, by the time the government troops arrived where we had waylaid them in hiding, we did not waste any time but we started attacking them. When they realized they were also in danger, they took cover, lying on the ground and firing very many bullets. As usual we let them fire until they were tired without responding until the time that they wanted to stand and that is when we fired aiming to kill.

We kept on playing that game of letting them fire too many useless bullets until the got tired and they started running low on their bullet supply. Just about that time, bombing planes started coming and hovering over us. General Kago advised people to flee the area as the bombing might clear the area of everything around, including all of us.

We escaped without the government troops knowing and we went up northwards for quite a distance from where they were. We could see from far the planes turning and bombing and the jet fighters pouring bullets like the rain but all this was a wasteful exercise on their side since there was nobody where they were targeting as we had already left the scene. We stayed up there until evening and we decided that it was unsafe to go back to our Bush and that we had to look for another place to put up our new camp.

We went downwards looking for a good site to put up the new camp and we identified one spot, which General Kago thought was very good and secure, as we could be able to identify the enemy coming from any direction. We built our camp nicely and even dug dungeons where we could fight from in case the enemy gave us a surprise attack. We also clearly identified any possible way that the enemy would come from. We lived in that Bush for six months and since we did not encounter any attacks or any problem while at that Bush it was honored and given recognition by being given the name of "Uhuru" (Freedom) Bush. We fought quite a number of battles while we were at that Bush but we did not lose any member of our troops. It was only one little fellow by the name of Mwangi Ngoci who had gone on his own to Kiburu to look for food and he was attacked before he got back to the camp. Afterwards, our food supplies started to dwindle and due to hunger, some people started losing hope and some surrendered to the enemy.

One day, twelve of us young men decided that we would escape from the camp and go up to Kiburu to look for something to eat. We realized then that we might die there in the forest if we did not come up with some innovative way to get food. The day we were making this decision was the sixth one going without having eaten any food. We left the camp in the evening headed for South Kinagop and at ten o'clock in the night we were at the farms of forest workers of Kiburu. These workers of the Forest Department had been forced to go back to their Reserve and they had left their un-harvested food on the farms. Their misfortune was our lack this time given that the potatoes were in plenty and we did not take long to get enough of what we wanted or that we could possibly carry. When we got there we found that the government troops had been there during the day harvesting potatoes—most of it left there in hundreds of bags. This made our task easy as we were able to carry as much as we could and also we poured out the potatoes and helped ourselves to the bags which we could later use to make tents in our camps. We did not take long there and we immediately went back to the forest towards our camp. We knew we had to stop somewhere in the forest before we got to our camp and roast and eat the potatoes and be back in camp before the other people started waking up, otherwise we could be punished severely if it was discovered that we had left the camp without permission from our superiors. The punishment would have been to be hanged because escaping from the camp without permission was considered a capital punishment that called for a death penalty (by hanging).

Once we got near the camp, we lit a fire and roasted a lot of potatoes while eating at the same time. We carried some of the roasted ones with us to the camp to eat on the days that followed. We spent the night there because we feared going to the camp with the potatoes because if we were found, this would put us with a lot of problems. In the evening, we went with our potatoes to the camp and each of us went to the usual place where they slept. It was each of our responsibilities to find out how to hide one's own potatoes so as not to let anybody else know except for those of us who had gone to Kiburu.

I used to sleep next to Kagera and Kariuki, both of whom were with me in Kiburu. We had left another man, our friend called Njuguna to ensure our belongings were secure. When we got there, we gave Njuguna enough potatoes for him to eat and some for him to store for himself and we all agreed that we would not give the potatoes to any one else because if we did there was the risk that those we give might tell to others and the news that we had potatoes might reach our superiors and we could be severely punished for it. We dug holes just around where we were sleeping to hide the potatoes and then we covered the area with some loose leaves such that nobody could know there was anything hidden there. What was really difficult was eventually how to eat the potatoes without being seen by the other people which was really tricky! You could not eat in the day because others will see you and you had to wait until night to eat. On the third day from when we came back from Kiburu, a man called Mwangi wa Makara saw me chewing since he was near our fireplace. He came towards me and begged me saying, "'Kamwana' (young man), I have seen you eating something and if you have some remaining, I beseech you to give me some and if you don't and I die of hunger, may you be cursed by this soil of ours that we are fighting for."

Given that I knew how hungry people were in the camp, I felt lots of sympathy for Mwangi. When I had the words he used to beg me, I told him, "Mwangi, I will give you some potatoes to eat. If you want to take me to our superiors and I be killed for having gone out of camp without permission, if I am killed, may you also be cursed by this same soil we are fighting for as well as by Gikuyu and Mumbi." Mwangi swore that there was no way he would take me to the superiors and if he ever did something like that, "may the God of the Gikuyu and Mumbi punish him severely."

I gave Mwangi a small heap of potatoes, which I did not know exactly how many there were but I would later find out how many they were after a period of six years. After parting with Mwangi, another man whose name was Samson approached Kagera and he begged him the potatoes in the same way Mwangi had approached me. Kagera also gave him a small heap of potatoes. When Samson left Kagera, he went straight carrying the potatoes to General Kago and within a few minutes, I saw our soldiers armed with guns coming for Kagera. He was not asked any question but he was pushed and kicked around as he was led to the superiors. At that time, Kariuki and I knew that we were in deep trouble as we had no doubt that Kagera would tell out the whole story and our names would definitely be mentioned. That would mean a death penalty for us by hanging.

When Kagera got to General Kago, he did not hide anything. He told it all as it was. He explained how we left the camp and came back with potatoes almost a full bag each back to the camp. Within a few minutes, the same soldiers had come for us and we were also taken in front of General Kago. We were asked to explain what we had done and we also told it all without hiding anything because we knew in our minds that even if we tried to twist our story or tell any lies, it was of no use because we would still be hanged.

General Kago asked us whether we knew the "law of self-defense," for that is what it was, that is, going out of the camp without permission, and we said we knew what it was about. At that time we could see that General Kago was really angry with us but since we knew that all the mistakes were ours, we were just asking him for forgiveness and we meekly told him how we would never repeat such a major mistake. However, even after pleading with him and asking for forgiveness, this was considered a very serious "crime" as far as the forest laws were concerned and so he still ordered that we all be tied together and be taken a few meters from the camp near the river and be guarded overnight awaiting a proper trial the following morning. He ordered that we should be properly guarded to make sure that none of us ran away.

They did exactly as they had been ordered to do and tied up all of us together. We were guarded overnight such that even if one would had wanted to escape, there way no chance of doing that. One man whose name was Karanja, who was armed with a revolver gun, guarded us and a few others armed with different weapons.

In the morning we were summoned to the place where cases were heard and when we got there we found the judge who would preside over our case; he was an older man who was very understanding and sympathetic. He would not let any of our people be hanged because he knew the many problems each of us was going through there in the forest. He also understood that in our case we did not go to Kiburu just for fun but much more because we were very hungry. That judge and six other old men heard our case. We were made to swear that we would never again commit such an offense and we also told them that we would never play with that particular law or any other and that we would be obedient and live by the laws of the forest from then onwards even if we would live in the forest for another hundred years.

That judge, as well as his assistants, was very sympathetic and they ruled that we should be taken away and be "jailed" near the Nyandarua Mountain. We would be fed from there and we were to be excluded from any future battles for a period of two years. It was ruled that if ever we were to be found away from the location we would be confined in, we would be arrested and hanged at once without any discussion.

We felt very pleased with the judgment because none of us knew that we could still be alive after what we had done. We could also note how saddened the people whom we knew closely were, as they also feared that we would surely be hanged.

Mr. Fillip Kimunyu was our judge. The other six men who were assisting him persuaded him to forgive us and not to sentence us to death. He however feared the reaction of General Kago who was looking very angry with this matter. It was a complicated situation. After the sentencing, the judged and the other old men took the verdict to General Kago and since he trusted those men, he just agreed with their judgment without any questions. Immediately after that, the traditional Seer who was entrusted in giving a leading visionary for all of us was asked to say where exactly we would be taken. The diviner consulted the spirits and directed that nothing bad should be done to us and that we should be taken where the judge had recommended and that we should have some of our soldiers guarding us day and night until that time that the traditional seer might consult with God to establish whether we should be allowed to mix again with the rest of our people.

General Kago ordered that we be taken at a place where there was a cave right at the foot of the mountain. He also ordered that on that day we should not be given any food and we should sleep on empty stomachs as part of our punishment. The following day, we could be given just a little food so as to really make us realize that what we had done was bad just because of our stomachs. We were to be deliberately denied food so as to learn our lesson the hard way so that we may never again think of escaping even if we got hungry. It was also supposed to be a lesson for the others so that they could see how they would also be punished if they decided to do like we had done.

There was no time wasted and immediately thirty soldiers led us towards the mountaintop, but we did not know exactly where they were taking us. Some of the ones who were leading knew where the cave was. It was about one o'clock in the afternoon when we left the camp and we did not reach our destination, at the cave, until five o'clock in the evening. Once we got there, we were ordered to get inside the cave and to stay there without getting out and if we tried to get out, we would not go anywhere as we would be guarded just as General Kago had ordered.

Inside the cave was really terrible as there was water dripping continuously from different spots and most of the floor was wet. One could not get any place to sleep or sit, as the whole area was wet. We stood the whole night long and none of us thought of going out of the cave because we feared the guards that had been allocated to us might punish us for doing that. We also did not know whether those soldiers guarding us were there or whether they had gone back to the camp. We felt cold, a situation that I had not been in before, but through God's grace, we went through the night and the following morning found us still intact and alive but extremely hungry and tired because of standing the whole night. It was two nights in a row that we had not slept properly because the night before our judgment we had been tied together and guarded closely to the extent that we did not sleep at all. These were tough two days that I could not eloquently express how we felt.

In the morning we tried to look around the cave floor to establish whether there is anywhere that one would rest. We were particularly looking to see whether one would find a stone or a rock inside that we could sit on. After a long search, since the cave was very big, we found a place that was dry and we could lay our tired bodies there. We decided that the dry place would be our new domicile for the time we will be living in that cave.

At ten o'clock in the morning, we were given food by our soldiers which was a glassful of maize and beans, so little that it could not satisfy any of us, especially since we had not eaten for two days. After giving each of us our food, those soldiers did not stay there but they just went back to the camp. As for us, since we had been freezing inside the cave for the whole night and that morning, we decided to bask in the sun and warm our bodies a bit before going back inside the cave. We decided that so long as we did not leave the cave area, just in case the General decided to come and check on us, we would be fine and we went ahead and enjoyed the sun.

We stayed out there at that cave for three weeks, and every day we were fed with a glass-full of "githeri" (cooked maize and beans) but from the fourth week, we did not see anyone come to feed us. After staying for two days without having any food, we felt that, no doubt we would die of hunger and since we did not understand why food was no longer being delivered to us, we decided to go up to the camp to check on what was going on. We needed to know whether our people were attacked and all of them killed or whatever it was. We left there walking very cautiously and ensuring that our own soldiers or the government ones, as in both cases we would have been in danger, did not capture us either. We kept going until we reached the location where the camp used to be.

When we got there, we did not find anybody, as all of them had left and we did not know which way they had gone. We circled around the camp for a while and what we saw was amazing as we identified no less than ten big holes that had been dug up by the bombs that were dropped by the war planes from the government side. We also saw different parts of our people's bodies that had been torn up by the bombs. We felt very sad because of the many of our people that had been killed during that attack and we were also afraid that we may never see any of the survivors if there were any. We were also not sure whether we would be reprimanded or killed by our own people given the fact that we had been sentenced to stay at the cave and told not to leave there without permission from our superiors. We were simply confused and dumbfounded for a while. We were concerned of what to do, where to go and where the next meal would ever come from. We were literally filled with much sadness and fear of what to do next.

Chapter 10

Our Fortune

We got at the camp at about three o'clock during the afternoon and we did not leave there until around seven o'clock in the evening. Since it had started getting dark, it was not easy to go very far, as the forest had become pretty dark. We tried our best to keep on moving headed towards Kwa Mwanya, and the following morning dawned on us before we got there. Given that we were still trying to hide from the government troops and administrators, we could not go to Kwa Mwanya once there was daylight. On the other hand, we knew very well that our troops had duty officers assigned to ensure security around Kwa Mwanya and if we showed up there, we could be easily arrested by our own soldiers. Since our sentence was still in place (that we should still be up in the mountain cave where we had been sentenced), being arrested near Kwa Mwanya would have made things worse for us. We therefore had to hide ourselves in a place that nobody could see us and we stayed there until it became dark.

Amongst all the twelve of us, nobody knew exactly where we were going mainly because we were walking only in the night and it is hard to note the major landmarks then. At times we found ourselves walking back in the opposite direction towards the mountain, and we had to make an about-turn downwards which made our journey very exhaustive. Because of the confusion we encountered as a result of the night travel, the following day, we were so tired and we decided that we would now walk during the day regardless of whether we would be arrested or not! We felt strongly then that if we did not do that we might die of hunger there in the forest constantly getting lost in the night.

We left our resting place of the previous night at about nine o'clock in the morning and we went downward at a place where there was a small river stream. As were walking strategically looking out for potential enemies, we immediately were able to sight a lone man who was quite a distance from us; we were almost positive that he had not seen us. We hurriedly hid ourselves and agreed that we had to know who this man was walking alone in the thickets of the forest. We waited for him to come by us as he was walking towards the direction of our hiding place. We wanted to take our time and verify whether he was alone or accompanied; we were able to establish that he was indeed alone.

When he got near to where we were hiding, we noted that he was carrying quite a large deer on his shoulders. One of us, Karobia, talked to him confidently, saying, "stand just where you are and do not attempt to run away because if you do, we will just kill you." That man was scared to death as he was not anticipating any other human being in this part of the forest, and as he was trying to come to his senses, the deer fell off his shoulders without his knowledge. He also fell down due to the shock he had just experienced. We jumped towards where he had fallen, looking almost dead, and we stood him as we quizzed him of his name, where he came from and what he was doing alone in thick of the forest. We were talking him cunningly and with lots of threat so as to scare him more. He informed us a lot about himself, mainly that he and three others were lost from their battalion and they were left wondering by themselves. Two of his colleagues later died as a result of bombs from the planes and he was left alone. Since the death of his two friends, he was just living alone in a cave adjacent to the stream, just near where we were and that when we saw him, he was going to his "home" in the cave.

After briefing us of his situation, we empathized with him, as we were all facing similar circumstances. We reciprocated by telling him about our encounters and the fact that we were also lost and hungrier than he was. This man was very happy to know us because he told that he had stayed there in the forest alone without speaking to any human being for five months. He informed us that he could not sing so as to practice his speech as he feared there could be enemy home guards or government troops who could capture him. For five months, our man had not talked at all!

We were filled with joy because of meeting with this man and after sharing a lot during the conversation, he asked us to go to where he lived so as to eat some meat that he had cooked previously. We had already told him that we had not had any food for five days. We went to where he lived and when we looked around, we liked the place very much because it was very secure. It was difficult to tell whether anybody lived there. He used to go up the river for quite a distance before he ventured in the rest of the forest. If by any chance he stepped on the river rocks with some dirt, he made sure he literary cleaned the rock so that no passer-by could identify any footmarks near or around the cave. Nobody could tell whether anybody lived there at all. When we got inside, we noticed that the cave was pretty big and this had become the home of this man for the last five months. He brought out cooked meat and we started to eat as we continued our conversation and we got full in due course. We asked him his name and he told us that his name was Ndiritu and he came from Nyeri.

We stayed in that cave for eight months eating game meat and sometimes we could get to Kwa Mwanya where we could get sweet potatoes. We did not like the sweet potatoes as much as meat because we could not store them fresh for as long as we could store meat. We still needed them though as an alternative diet to the meat. As you all know, eating meat every day was not the easiest thing but we obviously had limited choices.

There was a site we used to go, there in the forest, which was a bit clear, and we could see the horizons of the Reserve. From there we could see the government troops coming into the forest during the day to "hunt the Mau Mau." We could not then possibly wait for them to fight back because we had no guns. We retreated to our cave where we would hide until such a time that we could have guessed they had already gone back to the Reserve and we were then safe.

One morning, at about eleven o'clock, we went to that location that we used to sit observing the Reserve and seeing the government's troops entering the forest. While there, we saw some troops that were locally nicknamed as Njoni (Johnny's) at quite a distance coming towards the forest. We counted fourteen of them. We discussed amongst ourselves how we could outsmart them and steal their guns from them. After coming up with different ideas of how to go about the task we were setting for ourselves, we agreed that we could cover ourselves with the many dead leaves around where we were so as to disguise ourselves with the surroundings to avoid being easily identified. Twelve of us covered ourselves with the dead leaves.

It was clear from the way we covered ourselves completely with the dead leaves that no passer-by could identify us as we looked just like the ragged dead leaves surrounding environment. We suggested that the thirteenth person should go a distance ahead of where we were. His task would be to wait until all fourteen government soldiers (the Johnny's) had passed us and were now in the space between him and us. He was then to shout to them in a very loud voice, "HALT," which would make them all go down to the ground to set themselves for any attacks. We agreed that as they went down to prepare themselves, we would then rise and attack them snatching forcefully the guns they were carrying. Our man did exactly that and in a second's time, like the wink of an eye, we were all on them and each of the twelve of us had a gun. For the two government soldiers still with their guns and of course in total confusion, we pointed our guns to them and ordered them to drop their guns or we would kill them. They did not argue, as they could smell danger. They dropped them with ease and we took them. We ordered all of the fourteen to gather together in one group and remove all their clothes and any bullets, matchboxes, watches and shoes that they had with them. They did exactly that and they were left only with their underwear. We did not hurt any of them except one whose hand was cut by Gicheru when he could not drop his gun immediately as ordered. The hand was only cut once as he did drop the gun when he realized that he was in real danger.

We did all that in such a short time and within a few minutes, we ordered those Johnny's to run back the way they came without looking in our direction. They ran back almost in total nudity and we were very satisfied with our accomplishment! We were overjoyed when we now were in proud possession of fourteen guns. However, amongst us, only Ndiritu (the man we found at the cave) knew how to fire a gun. Everybody else did not know, as we had not had a chance to own a gun. It was more difficult for me and Kagera, who wound up with Stan guns while the others got rifles, but even them, nobody knew how to fire successfully.

After finishing all that we were doing, we knew very well that as soon as those troops reached their camps, government troops would flood the area in search of us, who according to them had done a heinous thing to the Johnny's. We knew very well also that if they found us where we were, we would have been killed without any question. We went up towards the cave and we got there around two o'clock that afternoon. A short while after we got there, we heard heavy sounds of planes which started dropping bombs for three consecutive days in the general area where we were. It was all a futile bombing exercise, as they did not hurt a human soul other than wasting their bombs.

We lived in that location for another two months and during this time, Ndiritu taught us how to set and fire a gun until we were all comfortable firing and ready to fight with the guns if there was a need. Ndiritu, however, warned us that we were not quite ready to fight the government troops with our newly-acquired guns as yet until that time that we would get back together with our own troops. A ritual of blessing the guns also had to be conducted by the witch doctor before using the guns to fight the enemy troops.

After two months, we decided that we should go out into the other parts of the forest and look for our soldiers. We figured that if they saw us with the guns, they might forgive and welcome us in their midst again as heroes. We discussed how we would prepare to leave for the journey to search for our comrades and we also agreed that we would move during the day and not during the night. We started cooking the meat that we would carry as food for our journey. This was usually game meet from the animals we used to trap with our homemade traps using the ropes of the forest. We wanted to carry as much meat as possible given that we had no clue when we might see the other members of our troops.

We cooked a lot of meat which we kept outside the cave but at around three o'clock in the afternoon there passed one small plane and it went over where were back to wherever it had come from. After a period of about ten minutes, many other planes passed by, this time just on top of the forest trees near where we were and within no time they had started dropping bombs. Some fell just a few feet below where we were cooking our meat. Immediately after that, we all went inside the cave to take cover from the numerous bombs being dropped. Within no time, none of us could hear what each was saying as a result of the heavy noise that came from the planes and the bombs. One of the bombs hit the big boulder rocks that surrounded the cave and many of those rocks fell to the entrance of the cave and shut it completely. We could no longer see the outside of the cave. All these problems we believed were brought about by the first small plane that passed over us when we were cooking the meat. It must have gone and alerted the bombing planes of exactly where we were which contributed to the heavy bombing we received.

After the heavy bombings and the loud noises succumbed, we tried to get out of the cave but unfortunately we could not due to the fact that the big boulder rocks had closed the entrance tight and they were too heavy for us to push aside. We kept on trying to get out, but it was all in vain. We continued to stay in the darkness of that cave for a full week. None of us knew which day it was any more given that it was constantly dark throughout the time we were in there. We finished the little meat we had saved in the cave, and we started getting hungry again. After staying for about another week inside that cave, we got so hungry that it was almost impossible to stand upright. We asked each other what we could do to save the situation but none of had a clear helpful suggestion. Just about that time when we were looking for helpful suggestions, Karobia suggested that since we were all doomed to die in the cave, we should start killing and eating each other, with the hope that a few of us might remain alive after feeding on the other's flesh instead of all of us dying of hunger in the cave. I felt very bad about Karobia's gross and inhuman suggestion (saving others through the act of cannibalism), and I told Kagera and Kariuki that we could not possibly do such a heinous thing so as to "save a few of us." I argued that even if we ate each other's flesh to survive the hunger, in the end the last person would also die like everybody else and therefore that suggestion would not solve the problem of all of us dying imminently. They fully supported my idea of stopping Karobia from carrying out his suggestion.

Indeed there was a lot of quarreling between Karobia and the rest of us especially because he had already targeted Gicheru as the first one that we could kill and eat since he was the stockiest. After quarrels and disagreements, he asked us what we wanted and what we could offer as a solution to avoid all of us dying. We told him what we were thinking, which was basically finding ways of digging with our hands and particularly starting with the small stones that had been broken by the bombs and pulling them inside the cave. We were hoping that the big rocks might tilt and fall as we pulled the small ones and that might hopefully open the entrance of the cave. Everybody supported the latter idea, and we started pulling the tiny rocks inside the cave. Karobia said he would not waste his remaining energy pulling the small stones as he knew that was a waste of time and that we would never be able to get out of that cave using that method. He gave us two days to push off the rocks and make an exit, failure to which he would start his stated plan, and Gicheru would not stay alive, as he would be the first victim. He categorically refused to push even a single rock.

We worked very hard, pushing the boulders on the side as much as we could. We were throwing the rocks inside the cave. We got so tired and hungry that as a result we could not speak to each other. We rested in darkness and after quite a while at a time none of us could remember, we started again and we threw more rocks with all the energy we had left. Just as the old Kikuyu adage that "Ngai ateithagia witeithitie" (God helps those who help themselves), we saw a miracle happening in front of our eyes. One of those big boulders slipped falling and almost crushed us, but suddenly we saw the light from outside. The hole through, which the light was coming into the cave, was small despite the fact that we had to squeeze ourselves through it to get out. Indeed the stones were bruising us as we got out. We left the cave one after the other, but Karobia was the last one to get out. When we all got out in the open light, a few of us suggested that we kill Karobia. They were still very angry with him for having suggested that we eat each other. Kariuki and I calmed them down and begged them not to do such a thing as murdering one of us. We argued that it was not our strength but the grace of God that had assisted us to get out of the damned cave hence we should not revenge on Karobia. God would not be happy with us especially after having saved us from imminent death.

None of us wanted to lay their sight on Karobia and some in our group started insulting him badly. He was smart enough not to answer back given the heavy tension and all intents to harm him by cutting him into pieces, had he answered back. We started looking for any remaining meat around the cave fire where we had been roasting. We could not find much as most of it was already rotten and the carnivorous wild animals had eaten up the rest. Whatever little we found, as rotten as it was, we ate so as to survive from the severe hunger we had been encountering in the cave. Given that Karobia was still afraid of us, he only ate after we all ate, meaning that his choice was the worst as bad as the rotten meat was. Ndiritu and Githutha went some yards away from us and after a while they came back with one side of a deer. They told us that we should go and get the other side. It turned out that this deer had been trapped possibly three to four days ago from some of the traps we had laid in the area for our food. It was not so rotten but the stomach parts as well some of the body parts were spoiled. We hurriedly went to get the other side and there and then, we made some fire using traditional sticks and immediately started roasting meat. We did not care whether the same plane that had sighted us before would do the same then. All we were concerned with at that moment was to get some food in our hungry stomachs.

We ate as much meat as any of us was capable of eating and we drank water from the nearby stream. We were now confident that we were out of danger from dying of hunger but only the possibility of dying from enemy soldiers from the government. We spent the whole of that day resting and sleeping, as we had not had any real sleep for many days, as we stayed awake from morning to evening. That evening, we thought of how we could get back with our people, and we arranged to leave the following morning in search of them.

Ndiritu told us that he was not going to accompany us in search of the other people. Instead, he would go back to his home in Nyeri. Since we all loved Ndiritu very much, we tried very much to persuade him to accompany us, but he refused. He told us that one day, he would come and visit us in our homes assuming that he would reach Nyeri safely and that he would never forget us. We bade each other bye and we also told him that we would one day go to his home and visit and that we would one day meet in the future. When we started our journey, Karobia was left behind quite some distance. I was suspicious that he may have been contemplating handing himself over to our enemies, but when I asked him what was on his mind, he told me that he wanted to go to Nyeri with Ndiritu. I called Ndiritu and told him what Karobia wanted and what my suspicion was. He agreed to travel with him and assured me that he would make sure that he would not allow him to surrender to the enemy as this would endanger us since he would reveal our hideouts.

We started our journey headed towards our home with full confidence that if and when General Kago would see us with twelve guns, he would be happy as well as the other people to receive us and to welcome us back. We walked all along that whole day until it got dark and we had to spend the night somewhere in the forest. The following day we kept going on up to about three o'clock in the afternoon. Fortunately, before we had even seen them, our soldiers, who were usually kept along the way to keep vigil for security reasons, had sighted us and had taken the news to the camp that there were people approaching and they were armed with guns. They could not tell from the distance whether we were "Surrenders," and usually if we were, they would have to overpower us and get rid of our guns. They would therefore need more support from the camp to wage a battle. General Kago sent his troops, about 100 soldiers. By the time we got near them we had no idea that we had been waylaid and suddenly we had a command for us to stop. Before long, we found ourselves surrounded by many men and in a speck of a minute, we had been snatched of our guns and two strong men held each of us tightly. It was clear that even if we had come prepared to fight, we could not have managed at all as we had already been outwitted and rendered helpless. We did not know that we were waylaid! We were not very worried of what had just happened because immediately we saw the dressing style of this people, we immediately knew these were our people and indeed we recognized some of them from the past.

Of the two people who were holding me, I knew one of them from before and his name was Kamau wa Mungai and the other one was called Ng'ang'a. I recognized Kamau by his voice when he ordered me to lay down my gun. I talked to him and told him who I was. I reminded him that I was Kamwana ("young man") which was my nickname. He also recognized me and indeed after a few minutes most of them had come to know us and they remembered well who we were. They, however, could not let any of us touch their guns, and we were escorted to the camp.

On the way to the camp, some of those who did not know us wanted to cut us up into pieces with their swords, but those who knew us intervened on our behalf and we got to the camp safely. Those who knew us remembered how we had been left in the cave when they were bombed and had to flee the camp they were in hurriedly after losing a number of our people.

When we got to the camp, General Kago interrogated us and wanted to be sure that we were not lying and that we were not Surrenders. He ordered that we be under close surveillance until the whole truth of our story is established. We gave the whole long story; some people were sent to where we had said we had stayed for the many days. They went there and verified the truth and when they came back, our story was now seen as credible.

When the authenticity of our story was established, General Kago was very happy with us and he recommended that we all be promoted to the rank of Corporal; and we were adorned with the medals for that rank. The medals involved sewing two pieces of leopard skin on the right arm of one's clothes.

General Kago called all of in the camp to assemble at our meeting place. He told us that we would go to invade one of the home guards' camps in the Reserve and that we should be ready any time when he would announce the actual day and time. We were taught more about how to use a gun than Ndiritu had been able to teach us. We felt confident about using the gun and were longing for the next battle. After one month, we were called again at the meeting place in the camp and were told that it was time to go and invade the home guards' camp that we had been informed of earlier. By that time, the foreseer had already blessed the invasion as "safe." We left our camp in the forest at about three o'clock in the afternoon headed for the Reserve but we did not know the exact camp we were going to invade. The reason we were not told exactly which camp we would be invading was for security purposes. It was to avoid circumstances where some of us may had have relatives or friends in the camp to be invaded and, being only human, may be tempted to alert them in advance of our plans. Attempts by one of us to alert their relative or friend would endanger our troop as we could find the other side readier that we were given the government support that they had. Obviously this would be tantamount to betrayal but there was a chance it could happen. As such, only General Kago and his close advisors knew where we were going to invade.

We went down southwards up to the Reserve where we arrived in the night. We kept on going under the leadership of General Kago and other senior military men in our group until we got to Gakarara School at about eight o'clock in the morning. Unfortunately, their guards and troops sighted us as we were going down hill towards Kandara. General Kago had divided us into three groups. The first group was told to go and attack from the southern side of Kandara; the other one was to go and attack from the road that comes to Kandara from Gaichanjiru and the third one, which I was in, was to attack directly into the Kandara camp. That's exactly how we were divided up and in a short while, we were right in the center of Kandara Boma. A trumpet was sounded and within no time, we were engaged in war with the home guards and the government troops. Since they had seen us earlier, they were well prepared and they had also called by cable to other neighboring government posts asking for assistance; we did not know that they had already called for assistance. Within a short time, the government troops that were there were as many as the leaves of the forest. The battle became much bigger than we were prepared for and in a short moment, planes started flying over us and some started dropping bombs and others tear gas, which we had no idea what it did, as it was the first time we encountered it. Our eyes became bitter and when you rubbed them, they became worse and all of us became semi-blind. When General Kago observed what was going on, he advised us to flee in whichever direction might feel safe. He told us that the battle had become much bigger than he anticipated and than the capacity we had. The sad part of this incident is that we were 600 of us and we had 240 guns amongst us and because of the tear gas, only a few were seeing what was going on and the rest had been blinded to the extent that instead of running away, they were running towards the enemy troops! It appears that when the tear gas was being dropped, the home guards and the government troops were instructed not to fire any bullets. That meant that as blinded as our people were, we could not know which direction the enemies were and this is why many were captured as they ran right into their arms. From the moment General Kago ordered people to run away for their safety in whichever direction they could find safety, I did not hear him again nor did I ever see him to this day.

As for myself, when we were told to flee, I ran downwards towards the valleys of Makindi River and went north running as fast as my legs could carry me. Behind me, I could see about ten people also running fast in the same direction that I was going. After going for a distance of about three miles, I found a place where there were young wattle trees that were a real thick bush and since it was the only place that was not open, I went inside and hid there in search of some rest. I rested for a while and then I heard footsteps of people running towards where I was and I immediately loaded my gun and got ready to attack. I decided that even if they were the enemies coming for me, I would make sure that before I died, I would also kill five or ten of their people. When they got near me, they stopped and when I looked from under the young wattle trees, I recognized them as our people. I used our "sign" for beckoning each other in the forest and they responded with the same and they came right to where I was hiding. They asked me, "Kamwana (young man), how did you get here and do you have any clue of how we would get back to the forest from here?" They also immediately informed me that General Kago had been shot seriously in the back and we would not be able to carry him as he was so seriously injured. We felt that carrying him with the intense of the enemy chase would not have been efficient, as it was clear that the General was going to die soon from the gunshot wounds. The explained that they had at least carried the revolver that the General had with him.

During such times as we had that morning in Kandara, nobody could really help the other as the situation was "everybody for himself and God for all of us." Everyone was running for his or her life given how bad the situation had become as the home guards and the government troops overpowered us. We stayed right where we were at the young and thick wattle trees until it was dark and safe to continue with our journey back to the forest. In Kandara and the surroundings, the place was under surveillance the whole day from government troop jets, which hovered above constantly. There were no bombs dropped especially because it was in the Reserve and amongst the people in the village, there were loyalists who could have been erroneously killed. They were usually helpful to the government when they revealed the hideouts of the Mau Mau, hence it was not in the government's favor to have them accidentally killed by random bombs.

When it got dark, the five of us who had been hiding left headed for the forest. We went upwards (north) using side paths as we could not dare use the main roads just in case the government troops and the home guards were out there looking for the Mau Mau. We climbed up and rested on the way. We finally got towards the main road at a place called Mairi and one of us, a man whose name was Githago, told us that he could now recognize where we were. At that time, it was about four thirty o'clock in the morning. We kept on going without any rest until we got to Kwa Mwanya where at least we could rest without as much fear as when we were in the Reserve which was heavily patrolled. We went up further until we got right next to the forest line and we looked for a "safe" place, away from the paths the home guards may have used. We were tired, sleepy and hungry from the long journey all the way from Kandara and we really needed a rest.

We woke up at about three o'clock in the afternoon, and we started harvesting some sweet potatoes from the neighboring gardens. After eating the sweet potatoes raw, we were also able to carry some which would be part of our food for the immediate future. We needed to go back into the forest where we could roast the potatoes, as we could not do that at Kwa Mwanya. It would have been too risky as the area was "a no man's land" and usually government troops were stationed nearby. Once we got into the forest, we roasted all the potatoes that we had and ate enough so as to be well fed to go and look for our people who had been scattered in all directions.

We left the place where we had spent the night very early in the morning headed towards Location 1 because we knew very well that if there were any survivors, we would see them along that ridge. In any case, it was also the same area that we had left those manning the camp. That was the only logical way for us to find out what was happening. We went on towards where our Bush was and found those we had left behind just in the same place. A few other people had arrived before us. When we asked them how they got there, they all had different stories to tell, some really surprising to us. It was also a sad day because many had been badly injured by gunshot and others had died. It was a mourning period for us. Other people would become disabled as a result of the wounds they had received. At the time we all met it was night and therefore dark hence we could not be of much assistance to each other given that we were all hurting one way or the other.

One man by the name of Ndungu told us of how one person they were with was shot and since he would not be able to carry the man and run away at the same time, he hid him in a tunnel that must have been made by animals. Since it was his leg that had been shot, he advised him not to make any noises to avoid the home guards. He promised to come for him the following day along with any others that may have been left behind in a similar way. Indeed, there were others, at least nine people who had been hidden in a similar fashion like Ndungu's friend. The location of some of them was known by those they were with, but there were also some who were by themselves and had hid themselves when the journey became too tough for them. In total there were nine men who were hiding along the way.

In the evening, about forty men were selected to go to the Reserve to alert our comrades there of the situation we had found ourselves in at Kandara. This was important because they needed to know just in case they saw someone with gunshots. They would have suspected him to be one of those in the Kandara battle and help him as one of us. When they came back they found five other men who had been hiding somewhere along the way as a result of their wounds being serious. After arrival at the camp, our doctors treated them.

After a day or so, people started arriving in small groups of fours, twos and even individuals. We decided not to move from there for some time until we were almost sure that there was nobody else still trying to rejoin the main group at the old camp. We did not want people to arrive there and start wondering where the main group went and get devastated after all the dangers and snares they had gone through. We stayed at the same place for another three weeks and within that time 510 had already arrived, and we felt at that time that it was unlikely anyone else was still coming.

We moved away from that camp and went upward north and went to another Bush, which was called Micharage-ini where we stayed for another month. Those who had gunshots by this time had nursed them and they were now feeling well. Nobody was sick from the injuries at this time, but we had to confront another enemy—hunger!

Those who had witnessed the shooting of General Kago briefed us of what had happened. We had been hopeful that he might have miraculously survived. At this moment, we gave up our hopes and came to the bitter conclusion that our General must be dead otherwise he could have by then joined us either individually or he would have at least come with the different groups that had joined us at different intervals. We were sad at this realization. We were also angry about the whole situation and concerned as to whether we would be able to get a replacement amongst us of a courageous and smart war planner as General Kago was. He had been an astute military genius full of tactics that had been very useful in the many raids we had carried out under his guidance.

We stayed in a situation of total sadness for quite a lengthy period and during this period Captain Waruinge and Captain Muiruri alongside led us with their juniors and the witch doctor (foreseer) by the name of Wandatu.

During this period when there was absence of a peace of mind, I started asking myself whether it was all worth it, that is, the many days and months that I had been in the forest. I wondered whether our new government would reward especially those who had suffered as much as we had in the forest. Would we be given back the land we were fighting for? Would freedom , "wiyathi," come to all of us? I wondered what exactly would be done in form of rewards that would make us forget the problems we had encountered in the forest. Would we be given land to console our many years of problems in the forest? Would our new

African-led government give us big jobs in offices? Would we continue to pay taxes like the poll tax, the hut tax, etc.?

When we got independence would be allowed to fight the remaining home guards who had been our enemies during the struggle? Where would the police and the army that had been our enemies go in the new freedom? Would the white man be allowed to remain and stay peacefully in Kenya given the way they had been brutal to the Africans?

These were questions going on in my mind, and there was nobody to answer them. I was just being troubled in my mind and imagining things. I had no idea what freedom ("wiyathi") was going to be like. I was not the only one who did not know the answers to my many questions. I was not the only one either of those in the forest who did not know what freedom or independence was going to be like. We were many who had this notion that "wiyathi" is something that would be given to us put in a container for all of us to touch and see. There were, however, some people who knew what "wiyathi" was all about, especially those who were older and also those who had been to other countries that were already free from colonialism.

Chapter 11

Micharage-ini Bush

Life got worse in the forest, and the home guards as well as the government troops surrounded all possible safe exits from the forest to the Reserve. That meant that we would continue starving in the forest as there was no way of going to the Reserve where we used to get food supplies. For over a month, we had no food at all and we started eating bamboo shoots and wild fruits like passion and other leaves that any one deemed edible and non-poisonous. One man by the name of Mwangi Ngoci went to the extreme by trying to cook the shoe skin and eat it. After eating the "cooked" shoe skin, he only lived for two more weeks; then he died.

Hunger and starvation continued to abet on us, and things were only getting worse. Some of our people started to hand themselves over to the government in desperation. Those who surrendered became our worst enemies as they could bring the home guards and the government troops right to our camps in the forest, as they knew all our ways. We were raided almost every day as a result of that cooperation that the government side got from our people who had surrendered. We stopped listening to the instructions of the witch doctor (foreseer), as they did not seem to make sense any more given the frequency that we continued to be raided. Everyone started to look for their own ways of survival and the troop/group unity that was there before started to break down. We also did not feel we had good leaders like we had before during the leadership of General Kago.

Without a courageous and a strong leader, people became disillusioned and started scattering in different ways. Some said they would go up to Nyeri where there were some famous Generals. They felt that if we continued to live on the way we were with constant daily attacks and no food, then all of us would die one after the other in a helpless condition. When our leaders realized what was going on, they thought of how the famous General Mbaria would come with his people and combine the two groups and assume the leadership for a bigger group. They felt they needed to call in General Mbaria sooner than later otherwise people would disperse in all sorts of directions.

Due to the frequent attacks that had become commonplace by this time, one morning the home guards and the government troops as well as bombing planes attacked us; over 150 were killed and others were permanently injured. Our witch doctor (foreseer) also died during this severe attack. The woman who used to cook for him whose name was Wanjiku also died along with five other women and one child.

When the people realized what had happened, they became very sad and disappointed. Everyone was searching their soul as to what needed to be done so as to have all of us speak with one voice. The disunity amongst us was starting to take its toll and could be partly explained for the big loss that we had just encountered.

Captain Waruingi and Captain Muiruri called the people to assemble in one place and told them: "The times we are in at this time looms a lot of danger and insecurity to our group. It is the high time for everyone to evaluate him- or herself and decide fully what they think they came to do in the forest and for what purpose. Those who wanted to betray the people fighting for freedom by surrendering to the enemy will be condemned. It is also the high time that they should decide to stay or to leave instead of continuing to put the whole group in unnecessary risks like the one we have just gone through. The cowards better leave now, as we will prescribe new codes that everyone will have to abide with. We will know the true patriots and the turn-coats amongst us."

Without wasting any time, Captain Waruingi told us that we would leave that Bush immediately to look for another place to stay. We needed to get far away from the daily attacks that we were going through. We picked up our luggage and started going further north towards the mountaintop. We were still without any spirit given what had just happened to our people. We were also annoyed as to the fate that had begotten us. After a long tedious journey, we arrived at a place that was open, without many bushes along the River Thika Valley. Since by then it was late and it was almost getting dark, Captain Waruingi advised us not to go into that open veldt until it was dark otherwise we might encounter an enemy there. We followed his orders and waited until it was dark to try and cross the open space.

Captain Waruinge and other leaders prepared for a ceremony to give people an oath that would ensure their solidarity with the group was unquestionable. The brave men amongst us encouraged the leaders to go ahead and administer the oath. Those who were rather cowardly had no choice but to go with the majority who wanted the oath. It was the oath of courage, and one that was to bring people closer and one that would unite them moreso as to be able to speak with one voice. We all declared ourselves to be fighters for our country's freedom and independence from the British colonialists. Once you drank the oath, you could now cross the open veldt to the other side. On the other side, Captain Muiruri, who greeted us by hand, symbolically tied up people in groups of ten with a rope. After that, still tied in tens, we joined the others who had already crossed earlier.

We had arrived at that location at about five o'clock in the afternoon; the oath administration went on until about eleven o'clock that night. When it was all over, we went up a bit and we were told that we would sleep at that location. We were instructed not to build any huts as we would be leaving the following day to go upwards more near to the mountaintop. That is where our new Bush would be built.

In the night, there were some people who were called amongst us to go and see our leaders. Given the way most of us were very tired, we did not even bother to find out what they were being told. All that most of us wanted at that time was to find a place and sleep and get rested for the next day's long itinerary. We slept being very dispirited and without much peace amongst us. We were hungry and had very little food stock. We did not have any idea where we would get more food given how tight the security around Kwa Mwanya was, and it was making it difficult to try and go to the African Reserves where we usually got our food. At that time we were around 800 men and thirty women, and we only had thirteen bags of corn with no other hopes for any more.

The following morning, we started our journey going upwards and northwards towards the tops of the Nyandarua Mountains until we were at the bottom of the mountain. This place was unusually thick with so many healthy and tall bamboos. We found the men who had been called amongst us in the night already in this place with lots of beef, from approximately five bulls. These brave men that we found there with the abundant meat asked us not to be worried as our God had blessed us with plenty of meat to eat and that He was looking after us and would not abandon us. They reminded us that we had a covenant with our God, that "He will not leave us alone for if we win it is not us but Him who will have won and if we are defeated, it is Him who will be defeated and not us!"

Everyone among us wondered where these brave men had gotten all that meat. We were also surprised to find so many people and at least twenty new people that we had not met before. We started putting our camp and this was an easy job given that there were many bamboo trees around there. By three o'clock in the afternoon, we had finished putting up different structures to accommodate different groups depending on how they got along or how many they were in a group. Some could stay in five's or six's. The smallest group would be of two people but nobody was allowed to stay by him- or herself.

After we finished our construction, we started cooking both food and the meat we found with those brave men; at about nine o'clock in the night people were able to eat and were about ready to go to bed. The following morning, our superiors called us all at the assembly point in the camp that had been chosen. We were introduced to the twenty or so new people. We were told that they had come from General Mbaria's platoon that had sent them to come and find out the truth about our General Kago. Was he really dead as they had heard or was he still alive? General Mbaria could not bring himself to believe any of the news he had been hearing about General Kago, whom he revered as one of the bravest generals they had. They were briefed closely about all that had happened and had led to General Kago's death. They felt terrible and regretted the loss of such an important leader in the war of liberation. They realized how his platoon and every body else in the forest would miss his wise guidance and wise leadership. His unique war skills would be missed terribly. They were requested to go back and inform General Mbaria the true facts about General Kago. They were also sent with a message to General Mbaria requesting him to come with his people and form one large platoon for which he would be the leader, as our people felt leaderless after the death of our General. Alternatively he was asked to inform us by emissary whether he would rather we join him ourselves, which our superiors were ready to move. They wanted him to be our General as we continued with our war to chase the white man out of Kenya.

Those people left to deliver our message to General Mbaria. We waited for his reply, as he was our only hope at that time. We kept waiting for General Mbaria's reply until we started getting impatient. From the time we sent those people, it took about three months before we heard anything from him. Our superiors felt that they should send some of our own people to find out what happened with our earlier message. Why hadn't he replied or sent anyone to inform us what he was thinking? We were also wondering whether the people we sent ever delivered the message as it was taking quite a while as we waited.

Sixteen of us were selected to go up to the Nyandundo Mountain and amongst us we had three guns. The old man Philip Kimunyu prayed for us. We said good-byes to our colleagues and friends, and they wished us well in our journey and the forthcoming search for General Mbaria. We were advised not to take too long and to come back soon and deliver the news. There was the fear that if we stayed too long, given the way the government troops and the home guards were constantly following us, we might find that they have moved from the location we left them. This would make it difficult for us to trace them, and yet they would be overly anxious to hear from us.

We went upward north until we reached the top of the Nyandarua (Aberdares) Mountains from where we could see all the different sides of our country. We could see the horizons of Nyeri, Murang'a, Njabi-ini (South Kinagop) as well as North Kinagop like the sides of Wanjohi. We could also see Naivasha from where we were standing. At the time we were enjoying the beautiful scenery of our country, it was about three o'clock in the afternoon and the sky was very clear with no clouds. This is why we could see all sides of our country from atop the Nyandarua (Aberdares). A man whose name was Koinange was leading us, since he knew that area pretty well. Before joining the freedom army in the forest, he used to be a squatter in Wanjohi, and they used to come to the forest and near the mountaintop hunting deer. He therefore knew exactly where we were at any time, and we felt lucky to have him as our colleague and guide. I found the mountaintop interestingly flat and level with shorter and fewer trees than down below. There were shorter trees locally known as "miruai" and other bushes locally called "matemani" which had thorns. I found the environment on the mountaintop very beautiful. I imagined how people could live there and nobody would know given that it was on the top, about 14,000 feet above sea level. The only thing that was not likable was the strong wind, which was literally whistling like a human being as it moved with great speed. The strong wind must have been coming all the way from the Indian Ocean without anything stopping it except the mountain, and here were on the top! We kept on walking until it was dark; as usual it was impossible to keep on walking at night. We looked for a place that had a small valley, which would be free from the strong winds. We laid down there and slept overnight. It was all peaceful as we had enough food, and we did not worry abouy any white soldiers coming up that far in the mountain at night.

The following morning, Koinange led us towards Nyandundo, and at about three o'clock in the afternoon, we arrived at that mountain. When we looked for any trace of a human being anywhere in the vicinity, we did not see any, and we felt the place had been long abandoned. We went round in many parts of the mountain looking for General Mbaria's people, but this was all in vain. We would come to places where they had been but you could tell they left the location some months ago. We looked for them for four continuous days, and we gave up on them, partly because we were tired and also because the food supplies we had were diminishing. We decided it was better to go back and report that we did not find them so that our leaders could decide what to do next.

We went back the way we had come, this time keeping a fast speed, as we all knew the way. Indeed the journey that had taken us three days to go only took us one day to come back. We got to the camp at about ten o'clock in the night, extremely tired and hungry. We did not tell the story of our findings that night; there were a few people who got to hear bits and pieces of our travel. The following morning we gave the story of our findings to our captains. They were not happy with us and commented that it would have been better to take a longer time, up to two weeks and at least find them. We were leaderless, hence the desperation to find the General.

The search for General Mbaria did not end with our return, and our leaders decided to choose two groups comprised of twenty people each. We were advised not to come back before we saw the General and his people. It did not matter if it took us a month but, the dire need was to get him and know where he was and at least take back his message to our leaders. We only rested for one day; on the following day, we were back on the journey towards Nyandundo to look for General Mbaria and his people. The group I joined was told to go back to Nyandundo and circle the mountain thoroughly up to Gita side, then up to the sources of River Mukungi in the search and onwards towards the sources of

River Turaca and Kinja and come out near Njabi-ini. If we did not see them after that thorough search, then we could go back and give our report.

The other group was to enter the mountain from the Valley of Wanjohi, going onwards to Ol Kalou and then to Ndaragua. They were to look for them all that side of the mountain and if they could not find them, they could come back to the camp to bring the news.

In my group, we had three guns. The main reason I was sent back again for the same search was mainly because my gun could not be given to anybody else. The governing rules concerning guns were that if the leaders had given you the gun, they could ask you to give to someone else. If, however, you possessed a gun because you fought for it yourself, or you personally tactfully or forcefully got it from the enemy, that gun was yours to keep throughout. You could give it to whomever you pleased at your own discretion. It was not because a leader told you to as nobody could ever do that. This showed respect of one's courage to earn his gun!

We went round the Nyandundo Mountain for over one week, and we did not see anybody. We could only identify locations they had camped and decamped. We could not tell to which direction they had moved. We later moved to Kwa Boru, and searched on all sides of the mountaintop like Turaca and Kinja. We went downwards also towards Njabi-ini; we did not sight them anywhere.

We were very tired given that we had been on the move all this time. We decided to stay on the "search" for another week. We figured that when we went back after two weeks and explained to our leaders about our intensive search, they might believe us this time. They might also give us some time to rest a bit.

We went upwards from Njabi-ini towards Kiburu where there were cultivated farms for the forest employees. There were no dwellings on these farms. Most of the people at that time who worked in the forest had been sent back to their original rural homes in Central Province. Others had been detained, while others were jailed for the alleged crime of having taken the Mau Mau oath. When we got to Kiburu, we harvested a lot of potatoes as well as lots of Soya beans as they were in abundance on these farms. Each of us carried as much as his energy could allow him to. We went upwards towards the mountaintop where we could not be easily identified by our enemies. The place we settled to roast our potatoes was facing an abandoned camp that used to be called "Uhuru" (Freedom) Bush. We spent the night there and the following day after we woke up, we kept on going further up towards the mountaintop where we were seeing both sides of the mountain towards the Kikuyu Reserve and towards Njabi-ini.

We looked for a comfortable place that we could stay for one week just like we had all earlier on agreed upon. It had to be a safe place where both our enemies as well as our own people in the camp who used to play the role of investigators could not identify us. If they saw us, then, they could have gone back to the camp to tell our leaders and we could have been in trouble with them. We could have been punished for having abandoned our assigned duties and coming back too soon. Before one week was over, six of us decided to take a stroll and visit our former camp, Uhuru Bush. We were curious to see how much damage had been done by the many bombs that had been dropped as well as seeing whether there was anything we could salvage of any significance that may have been left behind.

We went downwards for quite a distance. We were armed with two guns. Before reaching Uhuru Bush, we saw a human being that was not far from where we were at that point. We immediately hid ourselves to avoid being seen by the stranger. After observing the person for some time while in our hideout, we noted that this person was all alone and was busy concentrating on tying some wild ropes (miugu). When we observed closely, we learned that he was throwing the stretched ropes in a big hole that had been caused by a bomb. After throwing them in the pit, he tied one end on a tree and he went down the pit with the other end. Once he went down the pit, we rushed there immediately so that we could get there before he came out. When we got there, we saw him tying up a person who was at the bottom of the pit. When he turned up and saw us, he was terribly astonished given that he had not seen us earlier when he was busy with his wild ropes. He was so surprised and was tongue-tied, not knowing what to tell us since he was down in the pit to the extent that even if we were enemies, he could not find a way of helping himself.

Mr. Kagera was the first one to recognize the man and he told us that he was one of us and his name was Ng'ang'a. He called him with a loud voice and told him not to be afraid of us as we were not enemies. We told him to go ahead and finish what he had started to do before we interrupted him. He tied up the person who was in the pit with the wild ropes around his chest, just below the arms and using the rope that was tied to the tree he pulled himself up until he came back to the open. We assisted him in pulling up the man who was in the pit until he also came out. When he came out, we also recognized him as one of us whose name was Kiragu. Mr. Kiragu had been shot on his leg but fortunately only the muscles were injured but his bone was fine. His hand had also been shot but it was not broken despite the open wound. Kiragu was not able to talk due to his pain as well as hunger from the many days that he had not eaten. We later learned that he had been in that pit for eight consecutive days.

We did not go beyond that point. Instead, we felt that we should go back to where we had slept so that we could feed the almost-dying Kiragu. We thought that failure to feed him immediately would result in his death. He could not speak at all; instead of speaking, he was opening his mouth wide as if he was chewing something but no breath was coming from his stomach that could make him speak. We carried him up to where we were staying. We gave him the potatoes that we had roasted. He ate the potatoes very slowly, as he did not have the energy to chew. We were almost feeling like we needed to chew for him and feed him like a new-born-baby. He ate a small amount and then took a rest. We felt that was right because we also feared that if he ate too much, his intestines might burst given that they had shrunk a lot during the many days that he had not eaten anything. We assisted Kiragu in so many ways like washing him up and nursing his two main wounds with herbs from the surrounding area that we thought might be effective in healing him. We used such herbs as the leaves of certain shrubs and the juices from the "mutundu" tree and certain roots, all these based on our knowledge of herbal medicine that some of us had learned during our years in the forest. We were confident that his health was returning to normal and his wounds were gradually healing.

Ng'ang'a narrated his story to us informing us of how they were invaded by the enemy troops after we left them. They were scattered in all directions, and some of our leaders like Captain Waruingi and Philip Kimunyu were shot dead, as were many others. After being violently scattered, nobody knew where the others were unless you had run away in the same direction being in a group of twos, threes, fives or tens, or whichever number that may have formed a group. There were also those who may have escaped individually. Ng'ang'a explained how he was by himself and had been living alone all this time.

He told us that he had been living in a "very safe" place between two huge oak trees that had fallen a while back.

> The trees had a big opening in between, and I lived in that hole. It would be very hard for an enemy to find out where I was staying and it would take a lot of work and energy to split the two trees to reach the hole in which I was staying. I had trapped a deer two days after we were invaded, and I have been eating since then and I still have not finished the meat. When you people saw me at the pit, I had come from Uhuru Bush where I wanted to see how it had become after the bombing. When I was coming back to go to my "home away from home" I saw the pit and I curiously looked down and I saw a human being moving sideways. When I called out, he did not answer but I could tell he was not dead. I decided I had to try and remove him from the pit as I was in no doubt sure that he was one of us who had run away when we were invaded. That's where you people found me.

After finishing his story, Ng'ang'a excused himself to go and get some of the remaining meat from where he was staying. Kiragu also narrated his story that when people were invaded and scattered in all directions, he was shot and fell in that pit we removed him from during the same night that the camp was invaded. Given the pain he was undergoing and the fear that consumed all of them at that time, he could not remember how he fell into the pit. He was bleeding profusely and as much as he tried to climb out of the pit, he was unable to do it and hence the helpless situation that he was in until ourselves and Ng'ang'a stopped by. He lost consciousness as a result of the heavy bleeding. He just collapsed there in the pit and he had no idea how this all happened. He did not even know for sure how long he had been in that pit in that helpless situation. When he woke up and became conscious, he realized he had been sleeping on a pool of blood. The pit was wide enough, hence he moved a bit from the blood. He was, however, too tired and weak to try to come out and whenever he tried, he just fell right back to the bottom of the pit. He felt that it was God's mercy that we came by and rescued him because he felt he could have died right inside that pit. He was thanking us not knowing that indeed it was Ng'ang'a, who rescued him after seeing him down there. When he finished narrating his story, he started crying especially when he remembered where he had been pulled from. When his health improved, we took him to the pit to see for himself where he was desperately lying for eight days.

We stayed in that location for one month without seeing anybody from our group. We did not face any misfortunes like being invaded by an enemy. We also had ample food as we could always go to the Kiburu farms and refill our quantities of potatoes and Soya beans. After one month was over, we thought of whom we could reunite with the rest of the group. We figured it would not be easy to look for them. We went round the forest in all possible places that we thought they would be at but we did not find them. We did not see any footsteps that we could follow or signs of any recent human presence. After failing completely to sight them anywhere, we thought that they might have decided to go all the way to join General Mbaria in the Nyandundo Mountain. They may have decided that it was the best thing to do given that they did not have a General, only Captains, and now one of the captains had been shot dead.

We thought that it was better for us also to go up to Nyandundo because we believed that the rest of our group must have gone there. We figured that even if we went there and did not find them, we would look for General Mbaria's people and join them. The second alternative if we missed General Mbaria's people was to go up to Nyeri and look for General China's people, or General Hikahika's. If we found none of these groups, we were determined to go up to Mt. Kenya and look for other groups to fight with and to live with.

We started our journey headed for Nyandundo, which was a very tough one, given that we did not have enough food, as we would have wished. We went along looking for anywhere we could see cows or sheep belonging to the white settlers, which we could invade to get some meat. Unfortunately we were few and did not have people who could be sent ahead to investigate the area. We arrived in Nyandundo again and there was nothing new we noticed. It was still as abandoned as the other two times that we had been there in search of General Mbaria's people. We stayed there for a month, but we did not see anybody new. We decided that it was best for us to go back to our own area where we knew the ways well. From there we could head on towards Nyeri to look for other people to join.

We went back the way we had come but when we got to Kiburu, we decided to change routes and go towards the mountaintop as the Kiburu route was further southwards, and it would have taken a long time to get back to our destination. We went upwards to the mountaintop which took us a week from Nyandundo, partly because we were along the way looking for food and had invaded a number of settler farms. We had killed a number of their cows and sheep, which was now our meat and food for the rest of the remaining journey. At the time it got dark, we were almost at the side that we could see the Reserve but actually we were nearer Njabi-ini than the Reserve. From where we were near the top of the mountain, we could see down at the camp of the colonial troops; the electric lights and the vehicle lights as they moved in and out were clearly visible to us from up there. We slept somewhere in the bushes around the mountaintop. The following morning, we passed near where we had come from to check whether any of our people may have been back, but we did not see anybody.

While at the same spot, we saw two people who were familiar to us though we had not seen them for a long time, hence we could not recognize them at once. They were dressed in the same way like us and you could have sworn they were part of our group. When they saw us they came directly to where we were, and we greeted each other, as was tradition. They told us that they got separated from the other people after the invasion at the camp. They lived near Kiburu where they had stayed for three weeks as a group of eighteen people. They suggested that we should go with them and join them as we all prepared for the search of the rest of our original group. They were also of the idea that if we felt convinced that the other people may have moved to Nyeri, we should also go there and join them instead of staying without knowing what was next. They told us many things that were very convincing and made us believe in them; we all felt it was all right to go and join their group. We could all come with ideas on how to go about looking for the other people.

We went downhill towards where they had told us they lived. When we got there, we found the other people they had mentioned, and they did not mistreat us. Instead they welcomed us warmly and gave us the some of the meat they had and other types of food that we did not have. We ate and continued to converse with our newfound friends. We were also curiously looking to determine whether these people were really genuine and whether they had been living in this place for as long as they were telling us. Most of the evidence we had, for example, looking at old maize combs and meat bones led us to believe that indeed they had been there for as long as they were telling us.

Among the eighteen people that we met, we did not know about six of them but we knew the other twelve. We stayed in that location for about two weeks and at one time we went in a white settler's farm and took twenty sheep accompanied by our new friends. From that point, we were more convinced that these were genuinely our people and not turncoats. After the two weeks were over, four other men who were dressed just like us joined us. They narrated to us how they had gotten lost and were just roaming by themselves. That day we just lazed around narrating different stories, idling around until nightfall.

That night at about ten o'clock, Koinange and I went to the foot of a tree that had fallen, and we decided to sleep there. A man who was named Ngunjiri called Kagera and Gicharu. They went and slept there with a person that we did not know. Just about that moment, Ngunjiri and Josephat came to where we were sleeping and they were trying to find out why we had slept a distance from the other people. We replied that there was nothing amiss and that we just wanted to sleep there. Ngunjiri left and Josephat remained with us and within the time of an eye's blink, Ngunjiri came back with five men. At that time we figured that these people must be "Surrenders." We were not given any time to think or do anything as three of the men immediately jumped on Koinange and the other three on me and within no time we had been overpowered and floored down, and they had taken our guns from us. I shouted loudly so that the others could hear and those in a position to run away could do that. I called Kagera's name around and told these people were "Surrenders." Kagera replied and told me, "Kamwana, don't bother yourself because we were the first to be put down and were tied up before they came to you, so we are here being very helpless. We resisted for quite some time before these Surrenders finally tied us and contained us. Finally, however, they were able to tie us and they fastened our hands with metal handcuffs. They ordered us to wake up and go with them." I called Ngunjiri all sorts of bad names for his cowardly act of surrendering and now putting us in trouble. I told him I was not going anywhere and instead I wanted them to kill me there and then. We argued back and forth with them. They did not want to beat us and after some time, they took off and left us with four men. After half an hour, we saw many bright lights from a torch coming towards us. The one who had the torch shouted in Kiswahili asking, "Wako Wapi?" ("Where are they?"). When we heard that, we knew that was a white man, and immediately he came and ordered us to stand and get going!

Due to the great fear that the Africans had towards a white man at that time, we did not say anything. We just stood up quietly and followed those who were with him. We went downhill up to the road where we found two Land Rovers waiting for us. There were four other white soldiers as well six other unfamiliar Surrenders. We were taken and forced into the waiting vehicles. Each vehicle had three white soldiers, the driver who was white in both vehicles and two others in the rear. There were also two Surrenders in the back, all of them guarding us tightly. The vehicles started the journey, headed towards Naivasha and before we reached Naivasha, I discovered that one of those Surrenders was Ngunjiri. I felt terribly bad knowing that the next destination would mean being hanged by the colonial authorities. We had heard that if anyone was arrested with an illegal gun at that time, the sentence was murder. My own gun, considered illegal was right in this vehicle in the hands of the white people who had come with that rule, and it would be used as evidence against me. I felt I would rather they kill me then instead of taking me to be tortured more before finally killing me.

I looked at where Ngunjiri was seated, and I thought of how I would kill him before I was taken to my final destination where I would also be murdered. I marked well exactly where and how he was seated; I could tell he had no idea what I was contemplating in my mind about him. I decided in my mind that I would kick him very hard in his stomach by the liver and hopefully destroy it completely so that he could die and I may follow him after that. I prepared myself for the hard kick despite the fact that my hands were still handcuffed. He was sitting directly opposite me and within no time I kicked him very hard around his liver. Everyone who was in that Land Rover was astonished, as they did not know what was going on. Ngunjiri fell on the floor of the vehicle groaning and vomiting blood. The vehicle was stopped and all the white men came out with their spotlights lighting up the whole vehicle trying to establish what had just happened. They were obviously very furious asking what went on. One of the surrenders disclosed that it was I who had kicked Ngunjiri in his stomach. Those white soldiers decided that I be tied up against the vehicle, both hands and the legs as well. Those white soldiers did not rough me up. They ordered that one vehicle should be driven more speedily so as to rush Ngunjiri to the hospital in Naivasha. After the first vehicle left, we followed but we never saw them anywhere else even when we reached Naivasha. I later on saw those white soldiers at the "Surrender's Camp" in Kandara at a place that was known as "Gwa Kihiu."

When we got to Naivasha, the white soldiers left the vehicle and went to an undisclosed location. After half an hour they came back carrying bread and soda which they gave us to eat. It was at that point that my legs were untied. After we ate, one of the Surrenders was asked to return the soda bottles and, thereafter, the vehicle took off headed for Nairobi. We arrived in Nairobi at about four o'clock in the early morning. We did not stop in Nairobi; we sped through to Kandara, the final destination.

We met very many people, some that we knew and others that we did not and they all warmly welcomed us. The white soldiers ordered that we be given clothes and those who wanted to be shaved could go ahead and those who did not want to shave should be left to stay the way they chose. The also gave strict instructions that we should not be beaten.

We stayed at Gwa Kihiu for six months being tamed like wild animals. They were doing good things to us with the intention of making us forget the forest life or why we had gone there in the first place. They thought by treating us nicely, giving us clothes and food and not beating us, it would be a sure medicine to wean us back and to surrender to them as the likes of Ngunjiri had done before us. We were supposed to forget about the forest, and we were treated so well that we almost developed a feeling of no fear for the administration. Some of the people whom we had been arrested with found a way of escaping the Surrender Camp and went back to the forest. Those who managed to escape amongst our group had been taken back to the forest by the colonial authorities to arrest more of our people but instead found their "safe exit" back to the forest to continue the unfinished war against the colonial authorities. Those who fled back to the forest amongst our group were Koinange and Gicheru. After that incident, we were not allowed to go into the forest again as the authorities felt that we had not been fully rehabilitated to become Surrenders. Among the signs that made the authorities doubt our conversion were the facts that we had rejected to have our dreadlocked hair cut as well as our refusing to shave our bushy beards. We had also been constantly asking about our guns, and they kept lying to us that we would have them returned to us soon. We suspected these were mere fibs.

Ngunjiri did not die because after three months, he joined us at that camp. He never wanted to see me at all, as he hated me very much for what I had done to him. If we were not under scrutiny and strict supervision by the authorities, I do not know what the two of us would have done to each other, because I also did not want to see him at all.

We stayed at the Surrender Camp for six months. The white men who were the administrators there did not rough us up in any way. The policy of rehabilitation was to be nice to the Mau Mau fighters with the expectation that they would want to become "normal civilians" and discern the forest life. After the six months, we were asked to choose what we would want to do. The choices included being employed as a policeman or a home guard in the colonial administration, being employed in the coffee farms which belonged to the white settlers, or simply to be taken back to one's original home in the Reserve. People selected different kinds of employment as were being offered, and indeed they were employed. Many others, including myself, chose to go back to our homes and from that day I never ever saw my gun again.

Chapter 12

Fleeing from Detention

We were all loaded on to open vehicles ready to be taken back to our homes. When we got there, we were handed over to the local chief so that he could know and record our presence in his location. He was expected to keep a close eye on us making observations as to whether we had improved to become good "normal" people. He was also supposed to be our custodian especially charged with ensuring that we did not go back to the forest.

Our local chief was a very unsympathetic man as he hated the Mau Mau to the bottom of his heart. He decided not to let us go to our homes and, instead, he kept us on his camp where we were doing free manual labor without any pay at all. We used to dig and level the roads, fencing his camp as well as planting hedges. At other times, his soldiers took us to work on his private farms, digging and making terraces, planting Napier grass and other farm duties. We stayed at the Chief's camp for three months, and we were angry with him for making us work for nothing. Indeed we regretted why we did not choose to be employed like some of our friends who were earning something from their work.

One day we were to be guarded by an administrative policeman whose name was Kuhunya. He was to take us away from the camp where we had to get some posts to use to create shades for the young trees we had planted in the chief's camp. The policeman could never have suspected ill of us because he had by now gotten familiar with us and he used to trust us as he enjoyed listening to our tales of the forest life. He was fascinated with the kind of life we had led in the forest, and he believed he had gained confidence in us. There was an old man by the name of Kinyanjui who used to debrief ex-Mau Mau or those suspected of having taken the oath. He was working on behalf of the colonial government. He was a friend of my father, and I knew him before the war broke out as he used to visit our home coming all the way from Elburgon where he lived. He would stay at our place for about a week socializing and drinking beer with my father who also used to slaughter a goat for him. As kids we loved it when he visited because it meant we would eat meat more frequently. He also used to give us loose change like fifty cents, a shilling and all this made us very happy.

Mzee Kinyanjui on one morning called me in the office where he performed his debriefing duties. The chief was not there on that day. He told me that he overheard the chief saying that three of us would be taken to detention away from home. Those three included Waiyu, Waititu and me. He told me that he was sad about the prospects of my being detained. He advised that if it was possible, I should find a way of running away and going to the white settler's coffee farms where I could be employed so long as I did not consider going back to the forest. He also warned me never ever to say that he was the one who told me of the chief's idea to send us to the detention. I was saddened by the news this old man was telling me. I did not know how to possibly escape because we were guarded throughout, and it was difficult to escape. I now thought and considered it a God-sent opportunity to escape when we asked to go away from the camp to look for those posts. We went accompanied by our guard, Mr. Kuhunya, and we started our work of preparing for those posts. We were three of us, including Waititu, whom we were supposed to be detained together, another man from Kiria-ini whose name was Gakui and myself.

While we were out there in the bush working, I got an opportunity to tell Waititu all I had been told by the old man, Kinyanjui. I made sure that Gakui did not hear a word because we feared he might tell Kuhunya what we were planning. Unfortunately, or fortunately as it later turned out, he overheard us as we were talking and assured that if we were planning to escape, he would accompany us and would support us as we implemented the plan.

We discussed and decided on how we would grab Kuhunya's gun so that we could find it easier to escape. All the three of us jumped and overpowered Kuhunya at once. We warned him not to shout or blow the whistle if he did not want to die, and he saw that we were ready to kill him. Kuhunya just kept quiet without raising any resistance. We tied him with ropes against a large wattle tree next to where we were. We told him that we would just be near there where we tied him since we could not go very far during the day for fear of being arrested either by the regular police or the home guards that were all over the area. We told him that if he shouted for help or blew the whistle, we would just summarily kill him without any regrets or hesitation.

After tying Kuhunya and giving him all the warnings and threats, we did not waste any time there, and we started our journey to escape to "freedom" immediately without wasting any time. We decided to go up to the forest because we believed it was the only place that we could feel restful and "peaceful." We knew very well that when it got to be two o'clock in the afternoon, and we were not back to the chief's camp, the home guards and the other police would be sent out there to come looking for us. It was therefore necessary to go as far away from there as soon as was possible. We knew that once they came there and found Kuhunya all tied up, they would make sure that we were hunted from all sides before we escaped completely. We figured they would way-lay us on all possible paths they imagined we would take until they brought us back to book.

We realized that if we decided to go directly towards the forest, we would not make it to Kwa Mwanya before we could be arrested. We decided to confuse them and instead of going northwards towards the forest, we opted to go south-wards towards Kiriaini, which was also Gakui's home. Since he knew the area well, he could guide us as to where there were thick bushes for us to hide. It did not matter even if we took three days there in the Reserve. Indeed we figured that might be better for us because they might get tired and give up on us. This could help us as we planned the next idea of finding our way back to the forest.

We went downwards to the south hiding ourselves as much as possible. We passed in the bushes most of the time except in a few places that Gakui assured us that they were safe. We went on until we got near to Kiriaini and crossed on the other side of the valley in an area that had thick bushes of wild fern. We went upwards towards the top of the valley where we could see the other side and a vast area below us. From our vantage point, we could see the police and the home guards of Kiriaini going northwards towards Thare looking for us in the direction they thought we would have taken, but it was in vain as they were leaving us behind while they went further north.

We did not encounter any problems there because Gakui knew who our people were in that area, those who could feed us and inform us of any relevant news. They could also inform us of how we could connect with our people in the forest as well as telling us which ways were safe as we planned to go back to the forest. We stayed for a full week in that bush in the Reserve. Our people planned how we could be handed over to friendly hosts until we got to our people in the forest. We were first escorted and handed over to our assistants in Kagumo, who handed us over to those in Chomo, who in turn handed us over to those in Ga-tura, who in turn handed us over to those in Mbugiti who escorted us up to Kwa Mwanya from where we entered the forest without any mishap or misfortune. When we got back into the forest, we slept somewhere nearby. We were not worried as we had enough food that we had carried from the Reserve. We had hard maize combs roasted and salted and then applied on some cooking fat which ensured that it could take up to six months without rotting. One only had to eat a handful or two with some water and that was enough to fill you for some days. We had also carried dried roasted meat, which could keep us going for three months without going bad.

The following day we went up northwards towards the mountaintop with the hope of finding our people in the forest. It was all in vain as we did not see anybody. We could not even see any recent human footprints. All we could see were footprints of wild animals, like elephants. We went around the forest in various parts and sections that we thought we might find our people but we were not lucky. We did not see anybody. We did not even see any camp area that may have been recently abandoned. The most recently abandoned area was from four to five months prior, according to our estimate.

We regretted why we came back to the forest, but that would not be helpful given that we knew we had committed a big crime of stealing the gun from the policeman, Kuhunya, which would have led to a prison term if we were arrested.

We stayed for about two months in the forest, just the three of us. We noted that our food supplies were dwindling. We kept regretting why we went back to the forest and contemplated coming out of the forest carrying green branches which was a sign of peace and of voluntary surrender. We, on the other hand, thought that might be dangerous because once we give ourselves in, any punishment could be meted to us and we would be helpless.

We all agreed to go as far as the Nyandundo Mountain and double-check whether the people of General Mbaria had gone back there so that we could join their group. We figured that if we did not do that and our food supplies ran out, we might die of hunger there in the forest. We needed to be in a bigger group not just the three of us. We went back to Nyandundo where again we noted that none of the people from General Mbaria's had come back there. We could not trace any human footprints, and it was clear that nobody was anywhere there in Nyandundo. We stayed in Nyandundo for one week, and our food got finished. We persevered for two more days but on the third day, we resolved to hand ourselves over to our enemies as the only way of saving ourselves from imminent death.

We came downwards from the mountaintop towards the edge of the forest where we could watch discreetly the workers of the white settlers, herdsmen as well as the cattle and sheep flocks. We felt that we could not be able to wage any battle with only one gun. It also had only twelve bullets, just the way it was when we got it forcefully from Kuhunya, as we had not had an opportunity to use it.

While we were just standing and watching at the edge of the forest, which formed the boundary between the white settler farms and the natural forest, we spotted a woman carrying a load of firewood. She was coming from inside the forest but she was not seeing us. When she saw us, we called her politely like people who had nothing malicious. She kept her firewood load down and approached us up to where we were. We greeted each other with the traditional Mau Mau greetings, and she responded with the same kind of greetings which made us know at once that she was one our supporters who must have been catering to the needs of those in the forest.

We inquired from her a lot about where we were, how that place was, how dangerous it was for a Mau Mau and particularly whether she knew General Mbaria and whether she had a clue as to where we could get him. We also asked her whether there were other supporters of our people besides herself. This lady told us all about General Mbaria: how he had moved from Nyandundo to Nyeri and how that area had not witnessed any people coming from the forest like our-selves. She also told us how the colonial soldiers had shot her husband dead and she was left alone and continued to work in the white settler's farm. She offered us to stay at her place until the time we felt ready to leave. She informed us that there were very few Kikuyus who lived in that area. There were only four Ki-kuyu men, and she was the only woman, making a total of five Kikuyus. She informed us that she had three children. She also told us that one of the Kikuyu men was very bad, and those sympathetic to the Mau Mau could not trust him, as he could very well be a betrayer. She was confident that the other three Ki-kuyu men and she could give us all the assistance we wanted even if we chose to be employed as laborers on that white settler farm. She figured that each of the men as well as she could take responsibility of each other and sponsor them for a job on the farm. One could not be employed unless he or she was sponsored by one of the already established employees. We felt very happy and genuinely elated due to how this woman had been supportive and willing to assist us even further. We felt she was the true link to our support system. We later asked what her name was, and she responded that it was Tabitha Ng'endo.

Tabitha asked us to remain just where we were until the time she would come back which would be safe for us to go to her place. It was about four o'clock in the afternoon when she left. She came back at half past six in the eve-ning. After eating the food they had served us, we went further downwards headed for their houses, past seven o'clock in the evening with two other men. They brought us food and they invited us to go with them to their houses. They asked us not to be afraid as they could tell that we were not one hundred percent comfortable with them. They reassured us that all would be well and we would not be in any danger so long as we were with them as our hosts. After the meal we went further downward towards their houses. When we got to the place that had their camp and their houses, they told us that we would not stay all in one house. Instead, we were to be divided amongst three of them so that each would stay with one of the hosts. This was a precaution, just in case the home guards came to investigate the area to rid it of the Mau Mau. With the arrangement they had envisaged, they could easily claim one person as a brother. Since we did not have dreadlocked hair anymore and our beards were shaved clean, it would have been easier for the authorities to accept such lies. I went to Tabitha's, while Ga-kui went with a man whose name was Muriu and Waititu went with another man called Nyaga. When we got to Tabitha's, the first thing I had to hide immedi-ately was the gun. We dug a deep hole just that time in the night, wrapped the gun with nylon gunny bags and buried it there right in Tabitha's house.

We sat down talking about different things, especially about the war and the problems we had encountered, until very late; we were up until one o'clock in the morning. Tabitha told me the problems she had been given by the home guards who insisted on knowing from her the whereabouts of her husband. It was a very tough situation for her, but luckily she was not killed. She was tor-tured, and she somewhat survived.

By the time we felt it was now getting to be too late and we needed to sleep, Tabitha went out for a short call and while there, she found some people who were walking towards her house. She came back to the house quickly, but within a few minutes, those people came at the door, knocked and asked to be let in. She was not shaken at all, and she went along and opened for them. Five people dressed in army uniforms came in with their guns ready and pointed towards us. I tried to be courageous, but my mouth tasted salty as I wondered what would be next. I was thinking of all the crimes I would be accused of, like possessing a gun, running away and tying up a policeman back in the Reserve, knowing very well that these were government officers who had been looking for me. My whole body was shaking, but I tried not to show it externally—internally I was dying. They asked Tabitha who I was, and she told them that I was her brother. They asked me for an identity card, but I told them that I did not have one since I had just finished school. They asked me for my Movement Pass to show permission of travel from where I had come. I told them that I did not have a Pass either. By the time they came in, Tabitha had told me that if I was asked for my name, I should say, "I am Njuguna Kienje," which was also Tabitha's brother's name. And so when they asked me my name, I told them that my name was Kienje. We argued back and forth with those policemen and while we were still there at Tabitha's, the other two people I was with were brought in by some armed policemen. They were asked whether they knew me. Before we parted, we had all agreed that nobody would identify the other as if we had ever met each other. My friends said they did not know me and had never seen me. The man Tabitha and her friends had described earlier as mean and bad had seen us as we were coming to Tabitha's; he was the one who had alerted the white settler who owned the farm, who called the police who then came looking for us.

Since the policemen (army) knew that we were new there, they were not fully convinced with our cooked-up stories; they decided to take us to the house of the white settler. After we got there, the other people who had already claimed us as their brothers came over since it was not far from where they lived. They pleaded our case for us to their employer and told him of our problems and how we deserved to be left with them. He decided to let us spend the night on his compound. Our "brothers" and "sister" were asked to come the following morning to explain fully who we were and why we were there.

The following morning we went to the white settler's office. His name was S.H. Sherwin and he was a part of the Royal Family. He was asked by our "relatives" to employ us so that he could really believe we were related. He conceded and he immediately employed us as part of his squatters, which meant that one got a place to stay and had to work for the white settler. The salary was Ksh. 18 per month and raw food was included. We worked for him, and I became what was known as "shamba-boy," that is, a gardener, or one working around the house weeding flowers, etc. The others worked on the farm and also sometimes around the flower gardens and the maize plantations.

Since I was literate, Mr. Sherwin's wife found me one day reading a letter that had been sent to her from Eldoret, requesting for orange seeds to plant.

Most of the work on this farm was crossbreeding seeds especially of different fruits. She came right next to where I was without me seeing her. When I finished reading, I learned that the order that had been requested had not been delivered. I decided to put the letter in my pocket so that I could show it to Mr. Sherwin when he came so as to have the order processed. When Mrs. Sherwin noticed that I had put the letter in my pocket, she came to me and asked me to remove it and to tell her why I had done that. When I removed it, I told her the reason and she asked me, "You mean you know how to read?" I told her that I knew a bit of reading. She gave me the letter and asked me to read aloud so that she could hear my reading style. Since it was a simple letter, though in English, I was able to read it well; she was so happy that she immediately asked me to follow her into the office. I was immediately asked to accompany her into the office. She asked me to read a wall chart in her office, and when I did that convincingly, she immediately told me that I would be her assistant as the Secretary to the farm operations. That farm had 230 employees. I was given the employees' cards, and I was to write each employee's name and identification number. I was given an instant pay raise from Ksh. 18 to Ksh. 80. I was also given a house near the office, which was also near the Sherwin's residence. I had suddenly acquired an enviable position on the farm where the other workers felt intimidated by my presence. I was the one who was giving them their cards when they went to work every morning, and it was important to get it for without the card, one could not get the maize flour which was the main food ingredient. The person who used to give the flour was Mr. Nyaga, one of the men who welcomed us when we got to this farm as a friend of Tabitha. After they got their flour, the employees then gave me the card, which I would re-issue to them the following morning. While the other people got only two gallons of flour, Nyaga's, Tabitha's and Muriu's were not measured, and they could take as much as they wanted.

I was later able to remove Tabitha from the flowers in the farm to come and work outside the residence of the white settlers, which was easier work and less tiring compared with the work on the farm. She could finish weeding the residence flowers early, usually by ten o'clock in the morning, and she could have the rest of the day to herself to cook and stay with her children. I started thinking about the bad mean man who had alerted Mr. Sherwin about us which had led to our short arrest before we eventually got employed. I thought about what I could do to him to make him know that what he had done was wrong. I consulted with Nyaga and Muriu and they suggested that the best thing would be to make sure that he was sacked so that he could eventually leave that farm and go elsewhere. They were bitter because he had been reporting any new person and some had been jailed or sent to detention all because of this bad man. His name was Micharage. I thought of ways to make him suffer for all he had done to the other people and us. All I had to do was to plant something in him that would wrath Mr. Sherwin. Since Mr. Sherwin was from the Royal Family, he had the right to send to jail or prison anyone who had wronged him without going through the court system. He would not argue with a commoner. Indeed if you were found eating the fruits that he was growing, he sent the person to jail and ordered that he or she be sentenced to six months. This was done without any questions.

One day, I sent for the watchman, a Maasai whose name was Tutuma. I asked him to go to Micharage's house and tell him that I had ordered that he should go and work on that day in the forest harvesting "mareru" (some special leaves) to be used for wrapping fruits. I also asked him to tell Micharage that each of those harvesting these special leaves was expected to have four bags, which would be picked later by the farm tractor. Tutuma went and passed the message to Micharage. He did not heed the order since the forest job was much harder than the one of tending fruits, which he was used to doing and which was less tiring. He decided on his own not to go to the forest but instead went to his usual job in the fruit section of the farm. I had been informed earlier by some of the workers that there was man from among the Luhya tribe whose name was Khalaghaca who knew very well the kind of job (pruning fruits and spraying) that Micharage was doing. I learned that he could have gotten that job, but Micharage lied to the white settler that he was better than everybody else. I had already informed Mrs. Sherwin everything I was planning to do. I told her I wanted Micharage to leave the job at the fruits section for Khalaghaca who was better qualified. Sherwin's wife had agreed with me fully. When Micharage went to the fruit section of the farm, Mr. Sherwin chased him away unceremoniously and asked him to come to the office so that I could assign him other appropriate duties. Karagacha (the Kikuyu corruption of his Luhya name, by which he was popularly known) was called by other employees and asked to report to the fruit section. He worked with Mr. Sherwin who came to appreciate his knowledge of the fruit pruning, fruit cross-fertilization, etc. Mr. Sherwin was happy with Karagacha as he could work without much supervision, unlike Micharage who did not know much about fruits. When Micharage came to the office compound, he had a low opinion of me. He decided there was no order he would take from me and so he could not stoop so low as to come and ask me for an assignment. This meant he was also defying Mr. Sherwin who had sent him to the office. Instead, he went to another shamba-boy whose name was Wanyoike and started working with him weeding for carrots, cabbages, onions and other horticultural crops in that section of the farm near the home residence. I decided not to speak to Micharage but instead wait until Mrs. Sherwin came back from Naivasha, where she used to take eggs from the farm for sale on a daily basis.

When she returned at around noon, she came directly to the office so that we could enter the records for that day's sale. We could also make orders for the chicken feed as they had about 4000 chickens. We also kept the milk sales records. They sold nineteen barrels of milk per day, with each barrel containing ten gallons each. While we were in the office with her, she saw Micharage in the garden with Wanyoike. She asked me whether I was the one who assigned him that duty. I told her I did not, and I thought she was the one who did because I had assigned him to the forest task of collecting the special leaves, "mareru." I told her since I had informed her about the plans to post him to the forest; I did not ask him what happened when he came over there and started working with Wanyoike. Mrs. Sherwin was so angry that she called Micharage in the office and shouted to him asking whether he had gotten the message about going to the forest. He admitted that he received the message. He was then asked who had assigned him the job he was now doing at the garden. He said no one had assigned that job to him. Just as the two were talking and since it was during the lunch hour, Mr. Sherwin came in and found the exchange between the two going on. When the husband came in, he found his wife very angry, and he inquired what was wrong. The wife told him of how Micharage had assigned himself duties, and he was merely resting instead of working, thus cheating them on his eventual pay. Mr. Sherwin turned to Micharage and asked him: "When you left the fruit section, whom did I ask you to come to for an assignment?" He then answered, "the clerk." By that time Mr. Sherwin was angry himself and he retorted, "And then you decided to be your own boss and give yourself whatever assignment you pleased, eh!" Before he answered back, Mr. Sherwin closed the office and gave Micharage many slaps and kicks and roughed him up quite well until he was tired. He then placed a call to Naivasha police and within half an hour, a white police inspector, accompanied by six African policemen, was there. They were armed with guns and ready to take Micharage with them as instructed by Mr. Sherwin.

I sympathized with Micharage a little bit, but when I remembered that he had betrayed many of our people in the struggle, I decided that he deserved everything he was getting and more! Mr. Sherwin talked directly to that inspector of police and told him as follows: "By Her Majesty, the Queen Elizabeth II, I imprison this person for three years of hard labor for being disobedient to me and Her Majesty, the Queen." Nothing else was communicated to Micharage. He was simply whisked away and loaded on the Land Rover that the Inspector and his policemen had come in. He was taken to a prison which none of us got to know. Nobody bothered to find out where he was taken. Since he was not married, nobody on that farm cared much about him and indeed instead of people sympathizing with what had befallen him, they were happy about it.

Given that the white settler couple had come to trust in me a lot and they did not have any children there, they used to ask me a few favors. I did not know whether they had children in Europe or whether they had no children at all, as they were only the two of them and they were aging. They told me they would be going to Mombasa for a two-week holiday, and they were going to leave me in charge of the farm to run it just like they were running it. By then, they believed I knew almost everything that one needed to know to run this farm.

They indeed left as per the plan. When they were away after the first week, Muri, Nyaga and another man who was the Sherwins' cook, named Githuu, came up with some brilliant ideas which we all agreed upon. Githuu told us that he knew where the key to the safe in the house was kept. He thought there might be quite some substantial money in that safe. He argued convincingly that since we were all there in search of money, we should take the key and open the safe, share whatever money we would find and disappear from that area completely.

He also argued that since we did not have identity cards, it would be very hard for Mr. Sherwin or the government to trace us once we left the farm and the area. Mr. Sherwin had no clue where our homes were and therefore it would be difficult to trace us. We all agreed we would carry out that plan as discussed and agreed upon.

When we opened the safe, we found that it had Ksh. 30,000 (30,000 shillings) which was a lot of money then. We shared each Ksh. 7,500. We agreed that each of us should go to their rural home after sharing of the loot. Muriu's home was in Nyeri, while Nyaga came from Embu and I was from Murang'a. None of us was married; hence, we knew very well that without a family, it would be very difficult to trace us. We sympathized with Tabitha, and we thought that it was better that Muriu should go with her to Nyeri since her family was originally from there. We figured if we left her there, she would be arrested and asked by the authorities to show the whereabouts of the "brother" she had helped get employed and who had now been involved in theft from a trusting master and disappeared. We decided that instead of putting her in that kind of trouble, she should also leave and accompany Muriu towards Nyeri. We decided to share part of the loot with her and each of us was to give her Ksh. 1,500, thus she would eventually have Ksh. 6,000 just like the rest of us.

We arranged how we would make the escape from the farm. Nyaga, Muriu and Tabitha would go through the forest atop the Aberdares (Nyandarua) Mountains and come out on the other side in Nyeri. I told them I would go through Njabi-ini headed onward up to my home in Murang'a. At the time we were doing all this, the year was 1959 in December. When I arrived at Njabi-ini, I knew very well that if I went back home, I would be in deep trouble given the fact that I left there after tying up a policeman and stealing his gun. I knew I would be arrested and sentenced to prison for many years.

Before we left the farm, we called Waititu and Gakui, my friends from Murang'a. We told them that they had to think of how to run away from this farm. We lied to them that the white settler had come to know the real truth about us and that when he came back, we would be interrogated to tell the truth about ourselves. We also lied to them that the white settler already knew that we had stolen a gun. We intimated to them that the consequences we might face when the white settler returned was either to be detained or be killed. We made them feel things were really bad, and they had to do something in order to escape the foreseeable consequences. We pondered as to where we would take the gun that was still in Tabitha's house. Muriu offered to take it since they were to go through the forest. He said he would give it to our fighters if they met any during their journey in the forest. We told Waititu and Gakui that we had resolved that everyone should escape individually. This was to ensure that even if the government authorities arrested one of us, we would not all be in a group; and there was a chance that the others might escape such arrest and might become finally free. Both Gakui and Waititu went different ways and from that day, I never saw them again. I later on heard that Waititu was shot and killed at Eldama Ravine in the Rift Valley. I never got to see or hear about those who went towards Nyeri. It was difficult to hear about them, especially because I did not know which part of Nyeri district was Tabitha's or Muriu's home. Nyaga as well had not informed me which part of Embu he came from, neither had I told them which part of Murang'a I came from! I have always nursed hopes that we might meet one day and reminisce on the old days at Mr. Sherwin's farm and the way they saved us that ordeal night when the police came for us by claiming that we were their brothers. I have always asked anyone I have lived with or know from Nyeri whether they knew someone by the name Muriu, son of Ng'ang'a, or Tabitha Ng'endo, but no one has been able to identify them.

When I arrived at Njabi-ini, I decided that it was better for me to go as far away from my home as was realistically possible. I figured that if the chief from my home area knew where I was, he would order that I be arrested immediately and taken to him for discipline. I thought of how I would go all the way up to Kitale, a place I did not know and a place I had never been, far away from home. I figured that would be a safe haven as nobody could recognize me there.

I feared for myself a bit especially because of the amount of money I was carrying. I imagined being arrested on the long journey, but on the other hand I thought I might use the money to buy my way out in case the policemen arrested me. I thought that would be better than going to my home where I would most likely be arrested and detained immediately. I slept in the forest on the first night after we parted with the others. The following day at about six o'clock in the evening, I was at Njabi-ini. I boarded buses, which were owned by an elderly man called Gatimu. By nine o'clock that evening, I was at Naivasha waiting for the train from Nairobi, which would take me to Kitale through the Rift Valley. After many of us bought the train ticket, we waited for the train until eleven o'clock in the night. When it arrived, we boarded with haste and it left with its final destination to Kampala, Uganda. Those going to Kitale would disembark at Eldoret where they could change for the Kitale train. We arrived in Eldoret at four o'clock in the morning. We waited for the Kitale train, which eventually came. We arrived in Kitale the following day at ten o'clock in the morning.

Like the old Kikuyu adage says "weka wega niwe weika na weka uuru niwe weika" ("if you do good to others, you are doing it to yourself and if you do evil to others you are doing evil to yourself"). I found an amazing thing that I had never seen before when I arrived in Kitale. When I arrived in the town of Kitale, I overheard some of the people we had traveled with saying that they wanted to go and buy tea in the African restaurants instead of the Indian ones that were near the station. The African's food kiosks were near the bus station to the north of the railway station. I followed them since I did not know the town at all. Amazingly, the particular restaurant (kiosk) we entered belonged to the man I had given some potatoes to while we were still in the forest. It was on that day that I learned that the potatoes I had given him were fourteen in number. I could not recognize the owner of the restaurant, as he had grown big and muscular. He was wearing a very clean white overcoat as his work uniform. When I sat at a corner by myself, he brought me tea and he immediately recognized me without my awareness. He identified me with a special body sign that I had, and he immediately inquired what my name was. Since I did not know him, I was reluctant to tell him my true name, and so as he insisted, I gave him a fake name.

When he realized that I was not going to yield to give him my true name, he called me by my name; I was really surprised that he knew me. He asked me whether I had been fighting in the forest, and I lied to him and said no! In order for me to know whom he was and to believe that he knew me, he removed his overcoat and showed me a big scar on his right arm. He narrated to me reminding me of the location at where he was shot. He reminded me of where I was staying with Kariuki, and where he was staying with Mugo and how he begged me to give him what it was that I was eating (which was those potatoes). He reminded me of how Samson arrested Kagera, me and ten other people and how Philip Kimunyu interrogated us. He also reminded me of where we were taken at the cave for our sentence. He then told me how much the potatoes I gave him were and that's when I learned that they were fourteen. He told me that after that, he did not stay in the forest any longer because he realized that his wound was getting worse and he would die from it if he did not seek medical help. He told me that the wound was also very painful. He told me many other things that took place in the forest, which indeed made me remember him and recognize him and believe truly that it was he. He later called his two wives to whom he introduced me. He told them of how I had saved his life in the forest by giving him the few potatoes when he was almost starving to death given the many days we had gone without food. He asked his wives to make all kinds of good food for celebrations, as this was a remarkable day. It was like two people whom thought they were dead meeting alive again! It was an unforgettable day, he told his wives!

This man's name was Mwangi, and he already had four kinds of businesses on the same premises: the restaurant (kiosk), a bar, butchery and a shop. He also had a tailor at the shop. Mr. Mwangi told me about himself: how he left the forest and the only food he had for his long unknown journey was the few potatoes I had given him the night before. He went on up to Nyahururu, where he met someone from his home area who was employed as a squatter in a white settler's farm. He lived there for eight months hiding until his arm healed. He later learned that his cousin was the District Commissioner in Kitale for Trans Nzoia District. He asked his friend to give him the fare to Kitale. He gave him Ksh. 100 (one hundred shillings), and he used the train which was cheaper than buses as there were fewer buses those days. He went with God's guidance, as he did not have a Pass, which all Africans were required to carry, especially when traveling for such a long distance. He arrived safely in Kitale.

When he arrived in Kitale, he did not know his whereabouts, as it was the first time he had been there. After walking aimlessly, he heard some people talking in the Kikuyu language and he was surprised because he did not know there were any Kikuyus in that part of the country. He decided not to ask all of them as a group where the District Commissioner's office was. He waited and beckoned one of the people who looked more polite. He told me he asked him with respect for the directions. The person was a kind one and he showed him the way. It was quite near to the railway station.

When Mwangi got to the District Commissioner's office, he was refused entry by the Administration Police; the District Commissioner himself saw Mwangi from his seat in the office and recognized him. He sent his assistant to come and show me into his office. When he met the District Commissioner, he told him about his problems, and the District Commisioner assured him that everything would be all right. Mwangi told me a lot that I do not have to detail here. What was important is that he got the right papers that could allow him to live and work in Kitale, assisted by his cousin, the District Commissioner.

I also in turn told Mwangi all about me from the time we saw each other in the forest. I told him of the battles we fought, how General Kago was shot dead, how we went all over in Nyandundo looking for General Mbaria and his people. I also told him of how we did not find him, how we were arrested in the forest by some Surrenders, how three of us escaped after tying the policeman and taking his gun. Finally, I told him of how Muriu, Tabitha and Nyaga assisted us to get employment at Mr. Sherwin's farm and how we escaped the farm and each of us went to our respective homes. I made sure I did not tell him about the money we had gotten from Mr. Sherwin's safe. I told him of how I thought it was better for me to come to Kitale, a place far enough from home to keep away from our local chief who was determined to see me in detention. I told him I was looking for a job despite the fact that I did not have a Movement Pass (the pass-book was referred to as "bathi" in Kikuyu). Mr. Mwangi assured me not to be worried. He told me that I would get all the relevant government papers that would be required to legitimize my stay in Kitale. One morning, Mr. Mwangi took me to the District Commissioner to request a Pass to allow me to stay there legally, possibly to get one for a period of six months.

We went to the District Commissioner and he saw Mwangi outside, he asked his assistant to let him in. When we sat down in the office, Mwangi told the District Commissioner all about me, emphasizing what a nice person I was and how friendly we were to each other. He told him that I did not have a Pass and if possible, since I was looking for a job, he requested him to give me one valid for six months' duration. The District Commissioner was such a nice person and generous. He indeed gave me a Pass valid for six months. Mr. Mwangi told the District Commissioner that I would be staying at his house until the time I got a job. When I got the Pass, I was so happy because I did not even have an identity card, and I thought I could not get a Pass without one.

I stayed in Kitale for the six months, and my Pass expired before I had got a job. We went back to the District Commissioner and he extended it for another three months. Before the three months expired, that District Commissioner was transferred to another district and a new District Commissioner, who was a Luo by ethnic group, came to take over in Kitale. His name was Samuel and he was the contrast of the previous District Commissioner, as he was very proud. When we went back to renew the Pass, he said he would not give Passes especially to

Kikuyus who were there, as he believed all of them were Mau Mau or sympa-thizers of the movement.

I started thinking of how to go back to my home in Murang'a as Kitale was such a place that you could not live without a legitimate Pass. While I was think-ing about all this, one morning a man who lived in Endebess and whom I had met there in Kitale came over and told me there was a job being offered to work as a clerk in Cherangani Forest Station. I knew this was a job I could do, and so I went with this man, whose name was Zakaria Gathirwa, up to the station. We found that the Forester was a man from the Abaluhya ethnic group whose name was Lukibisi. He asked whether I could work as a clerk, and I answered him in the affirmative. He did not ask further questions, and I was employed immedi-ately. After three months he was transferred to Kimilili and a Luo Forester whose name was Onyango was brought to replace him. He asked me to show him my paper qualifications for the job I was doing and when I told him I did not have them, I was sacked from my job immediately. After I lost my job, I went back to Kitale, and I told Mr. Mwangi what had happened. I told him I was not going to stay in Kitale any more given that I had been there for quite a pe-riod and had no luck in finding a job. Instead, I told him I was now ready to go home. I thought that my local chief could no longer succeed in sending me to detention since the Emergency Laws had been lifted. The whole country was joyful as a result of the lifting of the Emergency Laws. One could now travel freely to any part of the country without requiring a Pass. This was a big relief. Mr. Mwangi persuaded me to continue living in Kitale, but I was also eagerly looking forward to going back to my home in the Murang'a Reserve to see how the place had changed all this time that I had been away.

I was so anxious to go home to see my friends and relatives. In particular, I wanted to be there to witness what would happen to the home guards. I was cu-rious as to whether they would integrate with the other people they had been punishing or whether they would go with the white people back to their homes abroad. I just wanted to see what the new Reserve would look like! Mr. Mwangi gave me the fare to go home for Ksh. 400. I had also saved Ksh. 250 from the salary that I got at Cherangani. I also still held tightly to my money from Mr. Sherwin's, and I still had a balance of Ksh. 5,800.

We said good-byes with Mr. Mwangi, and he escorted me up to the railway station. The train started the journey at four o'clock in the evening headed for Eldoret where we arrived at eight o'clock in the night. We left Eldoret at nine o'clock in the same night, arriving in Nakuru the following morning at eight o'clock. We left Nakuru at ten o'clock in the morning and arrived in Nairobi on the same day at three o'clock in the afternoon.

After disembarking from the train in Nairobi Station, I went towards Eas-tleigh where I knew a friend. When I got there, I noticed he was not there, and after inquiring from his former neighbors, they told me that my friend had been detained and they did not know where he was held. I had a very hard time be-cause none of the other people I knew were in the Eastleigh area, and it was now getting to be evening,, and nightfall was just about. I did not know how I would get a vehicle that would take me to my home.

I went back to the city center so as to think of a solution to my problem, which meant looking for a place to sleep or going home, if I found the right vehicle. When I got to Grogon, I met a man by the name Muneca whom I knew from before. He had lived in Nairobi for many years as a motor mechanic. We were very happy to see each other, as he did not think I was still alive.

Chapter 13

The Mau Mau Legacy and Its Relevance to the Current Socio-Economic and Political Situation in Kenya

This chapter is a commentary of the "story" of the Mau Mau Social Movement and its relevance to the current situation in Kenya, especially after a two year period of experience with a new regime, NARC (National Rainbow Coalition), and with a new president, Mwai Kibaki, following many years of oppressive regimes during President Moi (1978-2002) and President Kenyatta (1963-1978). By oppressive, I am referring to the perception held by the majority of the common man ("mwananchi") Kenyan who has viewed the previous regimes as those representing the rich and oppressing the majority of Kenyans who are poor.

The question this chapter will address is whether the interests of the Mau Mau from the many researchers mentioned so far (e.g., Lonsdale, Throup, Kanogo, Atieno Odhiambo) is purely an academic exercise or whether it has implications for policy in today's, and the not-too-distant-future, Kenya. I argue that whereas the Mau Mau was and will remain for many years to come an important historical event that dominated at least a decade (the 1950s), it is more relevant as an analytical tool to explain the social-economic and political gains of Kenyans to date. This is especially the case for the Kikuyu in Central Province and those in the Diaspora, albeit within Kenya, and to some extent even beyond the Kenyan boundaries. The aftermath of the Mau Mau and its impact on the nation's social change, more particularly among the members of the Kikuyu society in Central Province, is a subject of interest to sociologists.

Indeed one would use the historical materialism theoretical framework to explain the "the new social-economic" formations which were directly a product of the Mau Mau Movement. This framework mainly suggests that to understand the present, one must first understand who owned or controlled material wealth and ideology in the past. The historical analysis of certain periods as they relate to the present is key to understanding the social realities of any given society, and the Mau Mau period and its aftermath has not been fully analyzed from this perspective. The new social class formation in Central Province, the new social stratification and especially the new social class alliances were also directly connected to the "lost decade" (1950-1960), especially in socio-economic development of the Kikuyu society.

While the decade in question was particularly lost to those who were directly involved in the Mau Mau, especially those who went to fight in the forest, those who organized food delivery and medicine delivery as well as those who organized weapon collection and delivery methods, there are those who, to a larger extent, benefited from what was the "mess" in Central Province. Those whom without a doubt benefited from the "mess" were the loyalists, the home guards and any of the Africans (especially the Kikuyu) who were in the employ of the colonial administration. The sons and daughters of the loyalists, their friends and relatives were afforded many opportunities that were denied the majority of the Kikuyu people, especially those branded as anti-mzungu (anti-colonialists). They were afforded educational opportunities, business opportunities, civic employment and, though they were also targeted as enemies (rightfully so) by those in the Mau Mau, overall when the dust settled, they were miles apart in terms of actual material and personal benefits. Their position of being number one in achievement has not changed much if we took the overall picture.

I prescribe to the argument that if the Mau Mau Movement, *per se*, did not single handedly bring about independence in Kenya, it accelerated the pace and made independence in Kenya more of a reality for the Africans, especially those who had been in the Movement. It was able to destabilize the comfort of the British settlers in the colony to the extent that the British government started to see them (the settlers) as a liability and a direct expense from the Exchequer in London. Kenya was a troubled land in the decade of 1950-1960. The environment created by the Mau Mau preoccupied the colonial authorities, and the country was seen as if "it was on fire" hence could not attract investors and the agricultural production was decreased by the uncertainties in the settler farms. Indeed poverty levels, especially in Central Province, were very high given the lack of production as the preoccupation of both the government and the civilians was to contain the Mau Mau real or imagined terror threats. It was becoming expensive to maintain peace in Kenya and with the wave of independence in most African countries in 1960, the settlers' dream to remain permanently in Kenya vanished, and the British government was now willing to negotiate with the Africans it had all along referred to as terrorists (especially the Kikuyu, Embu and Meru ethnic groups).

Starting with the formal colonial appointments of chiefs which was often the highest administrative position Africans could hold (the lowest being what was then referred to as the headman, and later, assistant chief), it is very clear that those who occupied the most land were the chiefs followed by the assistant chiefs or the headmen and then the home guards. Land was the main measure of wealth in Central Province and it has continued to be to date. From almost all corners of Central Province, the story of wealth and large land acquisition can be told as uniformly true amongst the former powerful colonial chiefs. In Nyeri, for example, the wealth and big land acquisition of Chiefs Muhoya and Nderi are clear cases. In Murang'a, the wealth and land of acquisitions of such chiefs as Chief Njiiri and his son Kigo Njiiri, Michuki, Ignatius Murai (locally known as Inyathiu) Ndungu Kagori of Gatanga, Mwangi Mugwe of Ndunyu Chege to name but a few are clear cases of insurmountable land acquisition by individuals who were loyal, anti-Mau Mau, hence beneficiaries of the then status quo. In Kiambu, such chiefs as Njonjo, Koinange (even though the latter was detained as he was accused of supporting Mau Mau—but he had already made his acquisition by then), Muhoho and Magugu, to name but a few, all represent a select few who amassed wealth and particularly land in their localities which was not anywhere in comparison with the common man and woman neighboring them. We could add onto this but the main point is made here: the African/ Kikuyu colonial chiefs benefited enormously from their loyalty and oppression of the Mau Mau. It is no wonder some people would like to misinterpret the Mau Mau Movement as a class inter-tribal war (i.e., the landless Kikuyu fighting against their wealthy neighbors). That would be a misguided interpretation because the Mau Mau target was not simply their chiefs and the chief's cronies, but the colonial settlers and the colonial administration.

The questions still is: "What is the connection between then and now, and so what if the colonial chiefs benefited as much as I claim in acquisition of material wealth?" If we understand the simple theory "that social class regenerates itself and obviously makes sure it maintains especially the privileges and benefits it enjoys" then we can fast-forward the scenario during the Mau Mau Movement to after independence and to date. Indeed it should be clear by now that the chiefs and their cronies were acquiring that wealth to benefit themselves as individuals but also to ensure material security for their offspring. It is no wonder that the chiefs and their cronies (headmen to home guards and other loyalists) were able to take their sons (more so than daughters, who were not given a high priority) to government and mission schools at the expense of the sons and/or daughters of those associated or linked directly or indirectly to the Mau Mau Movement. Those that could not get schools in Kenya were sent to neighboring Uganda which had more African schools. Since there were no scholarships, parents needed money to send their children either to the mission schools or particularly to schools in Uganda. The sons of the loyalists, especially in Central Province, benefited from Western education which was to become the benchmark of upward mobility when Kenya became independent.

It is no wonder then that the children of loyalists (especially sons) were the first in many parts of Central Province to acquire some form of college education which was very well rewarded in the new African government. It was ready to reward anyone with some good formal education with various government positions which suddenly became vacant when the colonial government left in December 1963. Many of the sons of the former loyalists became the "who is who" in Central Province leadership. While this is easily generalized, there were a few exceptions where some lucky young men during their days had made it through schools and had attained what was otherwise reserved for the sons of the loyalists. The case of the late Dr. Gikonyo Kiano is an example of a non-loyalist son who made it through school and went on uninterrupted by the colonial social order of the day. Another prominent example is the current president, Mwai Kibaki, who like Kiano did not benefit from situations of many others of their time whose fathers were loyalists. Indeed, the prominent leaders of the 1960s and 1970s in Central Province in education, politics and economy read like a book of who's who in the loyalist camp. This could be verified virtually in every village then and now (2005) as I write this section. The trend has changed a bit in that there are more "self-made" men and women who have joined leadership ranks by pulling themselves from "their boot straps"—mainly through education or entrepreneurship and not because they have a background of parents or close relatives having been colonial loyalists.

A few cases to illustrate the point of how the children of the loyalists became "prominent leaders" after independence include the following: the son of Chief Njiiri, Kariuki Njiiri (educated partly in Kenya, Uganda and later the United States) became the first member of parliament for Kigumo—this was his father's and his brother's reigning territory during the colonial era; George Mwicigi Ndung'u (educated partly in Uganda and later in Canada), after having benefited from education facilities during the colonial era given that his father was a senior chief, became the member of parliament of the then Kandara constituency which included a big part of his father's former reigning territory. He was the member of Parliament for an uninterrupted ten years, 1969-1979. Other prominent names who were direct descendants of loyalist parents include the first Kenyan Attorney General, Charles Njonjo (educated partly in Kenya, South Africa and later the United Kingdom) and Arthur Magugu, a member of Parliament and former cabinet minister, to name but a few. Leadership in politics is not the only area that these sons of former loyalists dominated. Even in lower levels like middle level civil service jobs, teachers, bankers, etc. were areas that again sons and to some extent daughters of former loyalists dominated.

One may argue that this phenomenon that I describe for Central Province was not unique to and it happened in other areas of Kenya. That is not to be disputed; however, the extent of these divisions (loyalist and pro-Mau Mau) could not be more pronounced than in Central Province and parts of Eastern Province especially among the Meru. The situation in Central Province became more divisive after the Swynnerton Plan of 1954, which led to land consolidation and issuance of individual title deeds. Land consolidation, which was done when many of those in the Mau Mau were either in the forest fighting or in detention camps, became almost a direct benefit for the loyalists. They could decide where their land parcels would be consolidated; they could also deny or "allocate to themselves" land that belonged to others, especially their perceived enemies who did not have representatives to argue their case. It was the chiefs and the other loyalists who served on the Land Board who decided on land disputes; those who were centrally in the Mau Mau were always short-changed when it came to decisions on where land was to be allocated. The loyalists were also the first to be allowed to grow such cash crops as coffee and tea, meaning that they were also advantaged when it came to yields from their land. They were also able to get cheap labor especially from the many women who had been left behind with their children when their husbands went to the forest or were arrested and put in detention. Literally, they had everything going for them! They were almost as privileged as the white settlers benefiting directly from the administrative machinery of the illegitimate colonial government.

I argue most of the loyalists in Central Province, especially, were able to reproduce their privileged social class immediately after independence. They were earlier in panic especially in the late 1950s to early 1960s when they realized that those "Mau Mau neighbors" of theirs would be back in their midst. This may explain why Chief Njiiri was reported to have smashed the radio that announced that Jomo Kenyatta would be released yet the official propaganda up to then was that he and all the Mau Mau detainees would never be released and the white man was there to stay and rule Kenya forever. The official propaganda gave them the confidence to mistreat or steal from the non-loyalists because they also thought they would always be in power and in a privileged position. They therefore had cause to panic when it got clear that the Mau Mau detainees would be released and, worse, independence was coming. They feared retaliation from the wrongs they had done to their neighbors, and sometimes friends and relatives—or long before sworn enemies. They had either made them to suffer physically by beating them, or had lied to authorities to facilitate detention of those they did not like, or had allocated themselves land that belonged to those in the forest, or had through use of their power taken over the Mau Mau's former girlfriends or wives.

Their panic relief came when Jomo Kenyatta sided with the landed loyalist Kikuyus and preached the "gospel of forgiveness." This was to become the official policy after independence with Kenyatta becoming more comfortable with the loyalists and the landed Kikuyu reinforcing the social-economic positions even after independence. People were supposed to forget all the atrocities that had taken place in the lost decade, forgive those who killed one's relatives or those who took one's family land and move on as if nothing had happened that put one in a disadvantaged social position. Understandably the new independent government feared widespread revenge, especially in Central Province, would have made government operations difficult and it would have been like fighting another war. Of course not everyone agreed with Kenyatta on this one, and this may explain the early disagreement with the late Bildad Kaggia, then member of

Parliament for Kandara, a seat that the chief's son, Mwicigi Ndung'u, was to occupy a few years after it was made difficult for Kaggia to continue representing the area because of his disagreement with Kenyatta. The hopes of the landed Kikuyu were indeed as it turned out, that is, Kenyatta would become one of them, amass wealth and land and protect those who had already acquired as well as assure through freedom, "uhuru," the prosperity of their sons. Greet Kershaw sums these hopes and expectations when she writes:

> The landed were cautiously optimistic; they hoped that Kenyatta would continue to be a Kiambu elder in whatever he did. The only way forward was indeed freedom; freedom under Kiambu Kikuyu leadership was going to be their hope for the future of their sons. All agreed that Mau Mau should become a closed chapter of history for the sake of the future and for peace. This would not be easy but the past should be laid to rest.... Though harder for some communities than others, words such as Mau Mau member, Home guard, or loyalist were to be erased from one's vocabulary. (Kershaw, 1997, p. 259)

While what Kershaw (1997) is writing about refers mainly to a certain section of Githunguri, Kiambu, the sentiments and wishes expressed by the landed Kikuyu, the home guards and the loyalists were the same in every village of Central Province. There was an unofficial declaration of "mass amnesia" and anyone trying to remind the other people that there was a Mau Mau war and there were chiefs and loyalists who oppressed others and took their properties was to be seen as a traitor for the "New Kenya of freedom under Kenyatta." Again, when in post-independence a few like Bildad Kaggia, and later J.M. Kariuki, questioned the unfairness that had certainly set in the Kikuyu society in particular, they were dealt with unfavorably and strongly by the Kenyatta government.

The aftermath of Kenyatta's policy of "forgiveness" even when it was unfair to many became the panacea on which the future socio-economic and political leadership in Central Province and to some extent the rest of Kenya was built upon. The sons of the former loyalists (chiefs, headmen, home guards and those closely linked to the white missionaries) formed the first of the Kikuyu (African elites) in the New Kenya. The children and especially sons of these former loyalists had been educated when many others were denied similar opportunities. Their parents were well endowed economically and could facilitate upward social mobility. They also became politically linked to the new regime and were able to work their way up in seniority within the civil service or in private companies. The formation and entrenchment of these elites (most of them descendants of loyalists) dominated the Kenyatta era (1963-1978). Through social class reproduction, this continued into the Moi regime (1978-2002) and the same phenomenon is still with us in the Kibaki regime (2003-).

In the last forty years of independence those from the former Mau Mau families that have been lucky to get an education and were intellectually gifted to perform well in national exams have been playing "catch-up" with their counterparts from the former loyalist's families. The balance today is a bit of a mix, especially with intermarriages which have at times crossed those lines. Thus individuals (sons and daughters) of the former Mau Mau members have struggled to change the elite structure the New Kenya inherits from the former colonial set up and which was supported by both the Kenyatta and the Moi regimes. The Kibaki regime has a mixture of elites (self-made Mau Mau member descendants) and those from the "old money" (or sons and daughters of the former loyalists). This doesn't mean that all former loyalists' sons and daughters ended up in elite status in post-independent Kenya. There are individuals who did not succeed either because they performed poorly in their education, made poor business decisions or sold out their inheritance. There are also exceptions of the former Mau Mau members who had luckily made it through the education system and were also among the first elite formation in the new Kenya. The latter were more the exception rather than the rule.

This background and explanation of the current socio-economic class system in Central Province especially should be taken into account when trying to explain persistent poverty among many families in Central Province contrasted with affluent riches among others. In other words, the playing ground has not been level for all and the starting line was not the same for all and it was not by accident but by design from the colonial to the post colonial, to the present. The historical materialism perspective helps us to understand the Central Province society, especially its social class formation over time. The point here is not to raise people from the "prescribed amnesia" that Kenyatta endorsed. It is clear that even when people did not openly raise these issues, quietly they knew what was happening and whenever an occasion arose, subtle references were usually brought up. People did not totally forget but they played along for the sake of their own peace and that of their children as well as their neighbors. The point here is to give a valid explanation of the social stratification and inequalities that still exists in Kenya and especially in central Province—at least get to the root causes, which is important if we were to address those inequalities in a policy aimed at alleviating poverty and accounting for the differences as they currently occur.

Chapter 14

Conclusion

It is clear from the narrative (chapters 4-12) and the introduction section of this book that social change and development in any society—traditional or modern, colonized or un-colonized is a "dynamic and an inevitable process." It is a part of society and that is why it will forever remain a puzzling question as to which direction Africa's social change would have taken if she was never colonized. What would have been the fate, for example, of the formerly colonized Kenya and its fertile "white highlands"? Would such a violent movement ever have taken place if there were no oppression, indiscriminate extraction of material wealth and natural resources, humiliation and different forms of human rights abuse?

Like the social movements in France leading to the French Revolution which resisted the oppression of the Ancient Regime, the Mau Mau Movement was responding to an oppressive colonial administration and their African cronies in the name of chiefs and home guards. The Kenya colony had become a microcosm of British imperialism and its capitalistic ways to maximize profits at the expense of the natives. The natives were a people with a rich culture, a proud historical heritage and though mesmerized initially with the white people (butterflies as predicted in Kikuyu mythology by the seer, Mugo wa Kibiru), they were dignified enough to know their rights. It was only a matter of time before they resisted, and organized themselves into a social movement. The movement would inevitably become violent as all means of dialogue and negotiation were nipped at the bud by the colonial administration. Arrogance and superiority complex encompassed by the colonial state and its supporters (Europeans and Africans as well) led the movement willy-nilly into organizing a militant wing based in the Nyandarua and Mt. Kenya equatorial forests.

To organize the Mau Mau Movement and fit it within the large context of social movements (before and after), I note the significance of collective action, having goals for the Movement and resource mobilization to achieve the desired end. For those in the Mau Mau Movement, the quest for land, freedom or independence; the quest for education and free labor movements; the quest for human dignity, among others, were such a concern that those involved in the Movement could not understand why they had to suffer for so many years in the cold, dark forests. They realized, however, that the Kikuyu Reserve was by far less safe and more humiliating, hence, the choice to enter the forests and persevere—at least in the forest there was a feeling of "self-control" and designing to attack the enemy. It was clear for the forest fighters that even when there was defeat, it was something to live for and look forward to. It was at many times frustrating but there was also the hope of "freedom at last" and regaining of the lost lands that kept the spirits up and indeed kept the Movement alive and ongoing for the many years. As we can see from the previous pages, fear and hunger as well as disillusionment were part of the forest life. This is not to have been un-anticipated given the powerful government operations that the Mau Mau was juxtaposed against. The fact that those involved in it from the forest to the Reserve to the towns, like the city of Nairobi, were organized and had a sense of direction and clear goals giving lots of credibility to this social movement with many multi-faceted goals.

It is interesting to note that aspiration for Western education as introduced in Kenya by the Europeans had started to catch up as an avenue for social mobility. When the Independent Schools were closed, as in the case of Githunguri school, that the narrator attended, then most of the youth were left with limited choices but to join the Movement—as the only other hope. Those with little education were ranked a bit higher in the forest—as for example the case of Karari Njama who became the secretary to the War Council and was a personal assistant to Field Marshall Dedan Kimathi (Njama 1966). We also note that Muigai, our narrator, had opportunities of working as a clerk in Mr. Sherwin's farm after leaving the forest. Education rewards had been sought earlier and seen as a legitimate way to pave way for social mobility among the Kikuyu. This is why the people of Central Province did not take closing the Independent Schools and making it harder for the youth to pursue it kindly. During the Mau Mau period, the colonial education system introduced a biased system that favored sons and daughters of the loyalists. It is not a wonder that the earliest trained civil servants and those who filled many key positions when the country eventually became independent in 1963, were by and large the sons of loyalists and those who had embraced missionary Christianity. They were usually sheltered in the missionary churches and schools. The missionaries were seen as part of the colonial administration and their supporters were also by extension loyalists. It is not surprising that places like Kijabe, in Kiambu, Tumu Tumu in Nyeri, and Githumu in Murang'a (which became a Christian sphere dominated by the African Inland Mission) also tended to have more youth educated in their mission schools. The youth who attended such schools were mainly from loyal, Christian families (Sandgren 1989).

The activities of the Mau Mau Movement were deeply engrossed in the Kikuyu culture. Like all social movements, they (movements) do not exist in a vacuum and they are informed by the culture of the majority participating. Just like the Civil Rights Movement in the United States was heavily influenced by Black culture, hence Black Music and particularly the Southern Blacks, in the same way we note a heavy Kikuyu cultural influence in the Mau Mau Movement. This does not render it tribal or localized as Ogot (1992) argued. It only makes sense and brings the reality of a social movement by showing that movements are enlivened by the culture predominant in the area or region the movement takes place. The criticism leveled to the Mau Mau Movement, referring to it as atavistic because of engaging in Kikuyu cultural rituals should be seen as a misinformation and a misunderstanding of the richness of a social movement. The oaths taken organized within the Kikuyu traditions should be seen as the social glue that the Kikuyu could understand best. It was meant to unify the people so as to perceive things and what was happening in one voice. Initially, there was some success but in any movement, there will be dissenters and sell-outs that want an easier life on the other side of the movement. Many of the loyalists had been at one time strong anti-colonial activists, only to change sides because of their hope to reap more by taking on the colonial side. Understandably, it was a tough choice for many, especially those interested in property accumulation who did not think the "radicalized militant" way to the forest would be a good choice. They chose to stay in the Reserve and be promoted to "homeguard status, chiefs or headmen" with the aim of benefiting from the spoils of the Movement and the eventual war, especially in the years 1952-1957.

The organization skills and determination of the Mau Mau Movement participants challenge mainstream development theories, especially the "modernization theory," which blamed traditional cultures for the lack of "social change and development in Third World Countries." On the contrary, we can observe in the case of the Mau Mau Movement how culture was so important in organizing resistance. Culture was so much enjoined with the quest for freedom and outright and violent opposition to the colonial exploitation, which was depleting development, much more than it was encouraging it. I argue that culture here was used positively—first to reclaim the African (Kikuyu) dignity that was getting lost through the Western influence. Through song and dance revoking the traditional beliefs, the participants were reminded of their rich heritage and the need to reclaim and guard it—"die defending it if that be the case!"

Culture was also a positive influence to the movement especially because it became the basis of social networks that were so important—as they always are in achieving a successful social movement. Relying on clans, friendship and "riika" (i.e., age-mates) were critical elements in organizing Mau Mau Movement. The use of social networks in support for the Mau Mau Movement was reinforced through the many reminders in the forests and in the Reserve of the need for unity reflected through oathing, songs and dance, sharing meals and prayers and coming together as a united force. Their clear understanding of the need to free them and get back their Kikuyu dignity reinforced the determination that the groups in the forest had. So, traditional cultures in the case of the Kikuyu and the Mau Mau was not hindering development but instead prepared them for a Movement of monumental status that shook colonial Kenya right to its roots and foundation. This led the colonial office in London to reconsider the grip it had on Kenya and start negotiation with the so-called natives. Apparently in the late 1950s and early 1960s, the "natives" had come of age and worthy of the respect they had sought in the earlier years before the Movement started and became violent! So for the Mau Mau, there was an achievement in the long run at the national level with the coming of uhura (independence). At a personal level, there was not much achievement especially because they felt like the tables had been overturned and the loyalists had continued to do better in young independent Kenya. This was mainly because they were more prepared in education achievements given that they did not spend their crucial years in the forest like those Mau Mau fighters did. The basis of social inequality in Central Province to date cannot be divorced from the Mau Mau Movement despite the fact that it is now fifty years since the beginning of the violent phase of the Movement.

Overall, although many like the narrator in this book (chapters 4-12) ended up in more or less the same social class they were in before the Mau Mau Movement, they also expressed happiness in that they had freedom of movement and of expression. They were also and to this day, persist to be hopeful that their children and those of the next generation will grow up in a free Kenya, one without the political social oppression of the colonial administration and one that could give them equal opportunity for upward social mobility. The collaboration between me and the narrator is a testimony to the Mau Mau fighter's hopes in that a son of the Mau Mau fighters enjoyed growing up in a free Kenya able to compete in some opportunities that were previously only a reserve of the loyalists. Hopefully the next generation will go on to enjoy such freedom and now question injustices perpetrated not by the colonialists but by the new ruling Kenyan elites. It is for the present and next generation to think of ways of keeping the ideals of the Mau Mau Movement alive to fight any forms of social injustice. Social, political and economic oppression whether by the colonial regime or an African ruling elite should not be tolerated. It should become the basis of a new social movement, one informed by the past and borrowing from it with the sole purpose of bringing equal access to opportunities and reward for all citizens.

Bibliography

Barnett, Donald and Karari Njama. *Mau Mau From Within: Autobiography and Analysis of Kenya's Peasant Revolt.* London: Monthly Review Press, 1966.

Berman, Bruce and John Lonsdale. *Unhappy Valley: Conflict in Kenya.* Athen: Ohio University Press,1992.

Durkheim, Emile. *The Division of Labor in Society.* New York: The Free Press, 1956.

Fernandez, Roberto and Douglas McAdam. "Social Networks and Social Movements: Multi-Organizational Fields and Recruitment to Mississippi Freedom Summer." *Sociological Forum* 3 (1988):257-382.

Friedman, Debra and Douglas McAdam. "Collective Identity and Activism: Networks, Choices, and the Life of a Social Movement." In *Frontiers in Social Movement Theory*, edited by A. D. Morric and C. M. Mueller. New Haven: Yale University Press, 1992.

Furedi, Frank. *The Mau Mau War in Perspective.* Athens: Ohio University Press, 1991.

Gramsci, Antonio. *Prison Notebooks.* International Publishers Co., 1971.

Itote, Waruhiu. *"Mau Mau" General.* Nairobi: East African Institute Press, 1967.

Kaggia, Bildad. *Roots of Freedom, 1921-1963: The Autobiography of Bildad Kaggia.* Nairobi: East African Publishing House, 1975.

Kanogo, Tabitha. *Squatters & the Roots of Mau Mau, 1905-1963.* Athens: Ohio University Press, 1987.

Kenyatta, Jomo. *Facing Mount Kenya: The Tribal Life of the Gikuyu.* London: Secker and Warburg, 1938.

Kershaw Greet. *Mau Mau From Below: Oxford: James Currey*. Athens: Ohio University Press, 1997.

Kuumba Bahati M. *Gender and Social Movements*. Walnut Creek, CA: Altamira Press, 2001.

Le Bon, Gustave. *The Crowd*. Atlanta: Cherokee Publishing Co., 1982.

Leakey, Louis S. *Origins*. New York: E.P. Dutton, 1977.

Lenin, Vladamir and Henry Christman. *Essential Works of Lenin: "What is to be done?" and Other Writings*. New York: Dover Publications, 1987.

Likimani, Muthoni G. *Passbook no. F47927: Women and Mau Mau in Kenya*. London: Macmillan, 1985.

Lonsdale, John M. "The Moral Economy of Mau Mau: Wealth, Poverty, and Civic Virtue in Kikuyu Political Thought." In Bruce Berman and John Lonsdale, *The Unhappy Valley: Conflict in Kenya*. Athens: Ohio University Press, 1992.

Maloba, Wunyabari O. *Mau Mau and Kenya, An Analysis of a Peasant Revolt*. Bloomington: Indiana University Press, 1992.

Malthus, Thomas. *An Essay on the Principle of Population as It Affects the Future Improvement of Society with Remarks on the Speculation of Mr. Godwin M. Condorcet and Other Writers*. London: Printed for J. Johnson, in St. Paul's Church Yard, 1798.

Marx, Karl. *Capital Capital Volume One: The Process of Production of Capital*. Moscow: Progress Publishers, 1887.

McAdam, Doug, John D. McCarthy, and Mayer N. Zald. "Social Movements." In *Handbook of Sociology*, edited by Neil J. Smelser. Beverly Hills: Sage Publications, 1988.

McAdam, Doug, John D. McCarthy, and Mayer N. Zald. *Comparative Perspectives on Social Movements: Political Opportunity, Mobilizing Structures and Cultural Framings*. New York: Cambridge University Press, 1996.

McAdam, Doug. *Political Process and the Development of Black Insurgency, 1930-1970*. Chicago: University of Chicago Press, 1982.

McAdam, Doug. *Freedom Summer*. New York: Oxford University Press, 1988.

McAdam, Douglas. "Historical Context of Black Insurgency." In Douglas McAdam, *Political Processes and the Development of Black Insurgency, 1930-1970*. Chicago: University of Chicago Press, 1982.

———. "Tactical Innovation and the Pace of Insurgency." *The American Sociological Review* 48 (1983): 735-54.

McAdam, Douglas and Rucht, Dieter. "The Cross-National Diffusion of Movement Ideas." *Annals of The American Academy of Political and Social Science* 528 (1993): 56-74.

McCarthy, John and Mayer Zald. *The Trend of Social Movements in America*. Morristown: General Learning Press, 1973.

Morris, Aldon D. *Origins of the Civil Rights Movement*. New York: Free Press, 1986.

Ng'ang'a, D. Mukaru. "What is Happening to the Kenyan Peasantry?" *The Review of African Political Economy* 20 (1981): 7-20.

Ochieng, W.R. *A Modern History of Kenya, 1895-1980*. Nairobi: East African Publishers Limited, 1989.

Odhiambo, Atieno E.S. "Democracy and the Ideology of Order in Kenya." In *Democratic Theory and Practice in Africa*, edited by Walter Oyugi, Atieno Odhiambo, Michael Chege, and Afrika Gitonga. Portsmouth: Heinemann, 1988.

Odhiambo, J.A., M.W. Borgdorff, F.M. Kiambih, D.K. Kibuga, D.O. Kwamanga, L. Ng'ang'a, R. Agwanda, N.A. Kalisvaart, O. Misljenovic, N.J. Nagelkerke, and M. Bosman. "Tuberculosis and the HIV Epidemic: Increasing Annual Risk of Tuberculous Infection in Kenya, 1986-1996." *The American Journal of Public Health* 89 (1999): 1078-1082.

Ogot, Bethwell A. *Africa From the Sixteenth to the Eighteenth Century*. Portsmouth: Heinemann, 1992.

Piven, Frances Fox and Richard A. Cloward. *Poor People's Movements*. Atlanta: Vintage Books, 1979.

Rosberg, Carl G. and John Nottingham. *The Myth of "Mau Mau": Nationalism in Kenya*. New York: Praeger, 1966.

Sandgren, David P. *Christianity and the Kikuyu: Religious Divisions and Social Conflict*. New York: Peter Lang Publishing Inc. 1989.

Sidney Tarrow. *Power in Movement*. New York: Cambridge University Press, 1994.

Smelser, Neil J. *Theory of Collective Behavior*. New York: The Free Press, 1962.

Tarrow, Sidney. "States and Opportunities: The Political Structuring of Social Movements." In *Comparative Perspectives on Social Movements: Political Opportunity, Mobilizing Structures and Cultural Framings*, edited by Doug McAdam, John D. McCarthy, and Mayer N. Zald. New York: Cambridge University Press, 1996.

Throup, David. "The Construction and Destruction of the Kenyatta State." In *The Political Economy of Kenya*, edited by Michael Schatzberg. New York: Praeger Publishers, 1987.

Turner, Ralph H. and Lewis M. Killian. *Collective Behavior*. New Jersey: Prentice-Hall, 1972.

wa Thiongo, Ngugi. *The River Between*. London: Heineman, 1965.

West, Guida and Rhoda Lois Blumberg. *Women and Social Protest*. Oxford: Oxford University Press, 1990.

Young, Crawford and Thomas Turner. *The Rise and Decline of the Zairian State*. Madison: University of Wisconsin Press, 1985.

Index

About the Author

Kinuthia Macharia is Associate Professor of Sociology at American University, Washington, D.C., where he has been for the last nine years. Prior to that (1991-1995) he taught at the Sociology Department at Harvard University, Cambridge, MA. He was a recipient of the Fulbright Scholarship that funded his graduate studies at the University of California–Berkeley, where he earned both an M.A. and a Ph.D. in Sociology. He earned his first degree (BA, First Class Honors) from the University of Nairobi, Kenya. He was top of his class in both freshman and senior years, and as a result was awarded the Shell and the Ghandi Smarak Prizes for being the best student. Besides academia, he has consulted for the Government of Kenya, the World Bank, UNDP and the Population Council. He continues his interests in macrosociology, urban studies, the informal economy and social movements, among others.